Research Foundation Literature Review

ARTIFICIAL INTELLIGENCE IN ASSET MANAGEMENT

Söhnke M. Bartram, Jürgen Branke, and Mehrshad Motahari

CFA Institute Research Foundation

Statement of Purpose

The CFA Institute Research Foundation is a not-for-profit organization established to promote the development and dissemination of relevant research for investment practitioners worldwide.

Cover photo credit: nuchao / iStock / Getty Images Plus

ISBN 978-1-952927-02-7

Acknowledgements

Helpful comments and suggestions by Florian Bardong (SysAMI Advisors), Gurvinder Brar (Macquarie), Marie Brière (Amundi), Charles Cara (Absolute Strategy), Carmine De Franco (Ossiam), Giuliano De Rossi (Goldman Sachs), Marco Dion (Qube Research and Technologies), Kevin Endler (ACATIS), Daniel Giamouridis (Bank of America Merrill Lynch), Alex Gracian (Resolute Investments), Farouk Jivraj (Barclays), Bryan Kelly (AQR), Petter Kolm, Alexei Kondratyev (Standard Chartered), Christos Koutsoyannis (Atlas Ridge Capital), Jörg Ladwein (Allianz Investment Management), Ke Lu, Jon Lukomnik (Sinclair Capital), Spyros Mesomeris (UBS), Matt Monach (Aberdeen Standard Investments), Andreas Neuhierl, Raghavendra Rau, Berkan Sesen, Maximilian Stroh (Invesco), Scott Taylor (AIG), Simon Taylor, Argyris Tsiaras, Nir Vulkan (Oxford Man Institute), Markos Zachariadis, Riccardo Zecchinelli (UK Cabinet Office), and seminar participants at 13th Financial Risks International Forum, 2020 CERF in the City Conference, 2020 WBS Investment Challenge, Barclays Quantitative Investment Strategies (QIS) group, Cambridge Judge Business School, the 13th Financial Risks International Forum, and the 2020 Paris Conference on FinTech and Cryptofinance are gratefully acknowledged. Söhnke Bartram gratefully acknowledges the warm hospitality of Cambridge University, Fudan University, and Oxford University.

Contents

PL Qualified Activity CFA Institute

This publication qualifies for 1.5 PL credits under the guidelines of the CFA Institute Professional Learning Program.

Artificial Intelligence in Asset Management

Söhnke M. Bartram
Research Fellow, Centre for Economic Policy Research, and Professor of Finance, University of Warwick, Warwick Business School, Department of Finance

Jürgen Branke
Professor of Operational Research and Systems, University of Warwick, Warwick Business School

Mehrshad Motahari
Research Associate, Cambridge Centre for Finance and Cambridge Endowment for Research in Finance, University of Cambridge, Cambridge Judge Business School

1. Introduction

Artificial intelligence (AI) is one of the hottest topics of current times because it has disrupted most industries in recent years, and the financial services sector is no exception. With the advent of fintech, which has a particular emphasis on AI, the sector has experienced a revolution in some of its core practices. Probably the most affected area is asset management, which is expected to suffer the largest number of job cuts in the near future (Buchanan 2019). A sizable proportion of asset management companies are now using AI and statistical models to run trading and investment platforms. The increased use of AI across a range of tasks in asset management calls for a more systematic examination of the various techniques and applications involved, as well as the concomitant opportunities and challenges they bring to the sector.

This study provides a comprehensive overview of a wide range of existing and emerging applications of AI in asset management, highlighting the key topics of debate. We focus on three major areas: portfolio management, trading, and portfolio risk management. Portfolio management entails making asset allocation decisions to construct a portfolio with specific risk and return characteristics. AI techniques can contribute to this process by facilitating fundamental analysis through quantitative or textual data analysis and generating novel investment strategies. AI techniques can also help improve the shortcomings of classical portfolio construction techniques. In particular, AI can produce better asset return and risk estimates and solve portfolio optimization problems with complex constraints, yielding portfolios with better out-of-sample performance compared with traditional approaches.

Trading is another popular area for AI applications. Considering the growing speed and complexity of trades, AI techniques are becoming an essential part of trading practice. A particularly attractive feature of AI is its ability to process large amounts of data to generate trading signals. Algorithms can be trained to automatically execute trades based on these signals, which has given rise to the industry of algorithmic (or algo) trading. In addition, AI techniques can reduce transaction costs by automatically analyzing the market and subsequently identifying the best time, size, and venue for trades.

AI also has vast implications for portfolio risk management. Since the 2008 global financial crisis, risk management and compliance have been at the forefront of asset management practices. With financial assets and global markets becoming increasingly complex, traditional risk models may no longer be sufficient for risk analysis. At the same time, AI techniques that learn and evolve by using data can provide additional tools for monitoring risk. Specifically, AI assists risk managers in validating and backtesting risk models. AI approaches can also extract information more efficiently from various sources of structured or unstructured data and generate more accurate forecasts of bankruptcy and credit risk, market volatility, macroeconomic trends, financial crises, and so on than traditional techniques.

Furthermore, robo-advising has gained significant public interest in recent years. Robo-advisors are computer programs that provide digital financial investment advice based on mathematical rules or algorithms tailored to investors' needs and preferences. The popularity of robo-advisors stems from their success in democratizing investment advisory services by making them cheaper and more accessible to unsophisticated individual investors. Robo-advisors are particularly attractive to young and tech-savvy investors, such as Generation Y (millennials). AI is the backbone of typical robo-advising algorithms, which rely heavily on the application of AI across all dimensions of asset management.

We also discuss a number of possible disadvantages of using AI in asset management. AI models are often opaque and complex, making them difficult for managers to monitor and scrutinize. The models' reliance on and sensitivity to data can introduce a considerable source of risk. AI models can be improperly trained as a result of using poor-quality or insufficient data. Ineffective human supervision might lead to systematic crashes, an inability to identify inference errors, and a lack of understanding of investment practices and performance attribution by investors. Lastly, whether the benefits associated with AI can justify its considerable development and implementation cost is unclear.

The remainder of the piece is organized as follows. Section 2 provides an overview of trends in AI and of the most common AI techniques used in asset management. AI applications in portfolio management, trading, and portfolio risk management are discussed in Sections 3, 4, and 5, respectively. Section 6 covers the use of AI in robo-advising, and Section 7 discusses some of the risks and concerns associated with AI. Section 8 concludes with a summary of the main takeaways.

2. Trends in Artificial Intelligence

In recent years, the popularity of AI in general—and of machine learning (ML) specifically—has surged in both practice and academia. Consequently, the number of research papers published with the keywords "artificial intelligence" and "machine learning" has increased dramatically in the past five years (**Figure 1**). AI is a broader concept than ML, because it refers to the general use of computers to imitate human cognitive functions. ML is effectively a subset of AI, in which machines are able to decide and perform actions based on past experiences. To date, AI applications in finance mostly make use of ML techniques, such as statistical learning, and thus the AI label applies only in a very broad sense (e.g., Gu, Kelly, and Xiu 2020). Moreover, a large part of what is branded as AI (or ML) in finance is not new but has existed in the form of statistical or econometric modeling techniques for a long time.

The recent hype about AI can be attributed to three developments that are not necessarily related to the science of AI itself (Giamouridis 2017). First, computer processing and storage capacity have improved remarkably in the past decade, making the use of some longstanding AI techniques feasible.

Figure 1. Number of Published Research Papers by Topic over Time, 1996–2018

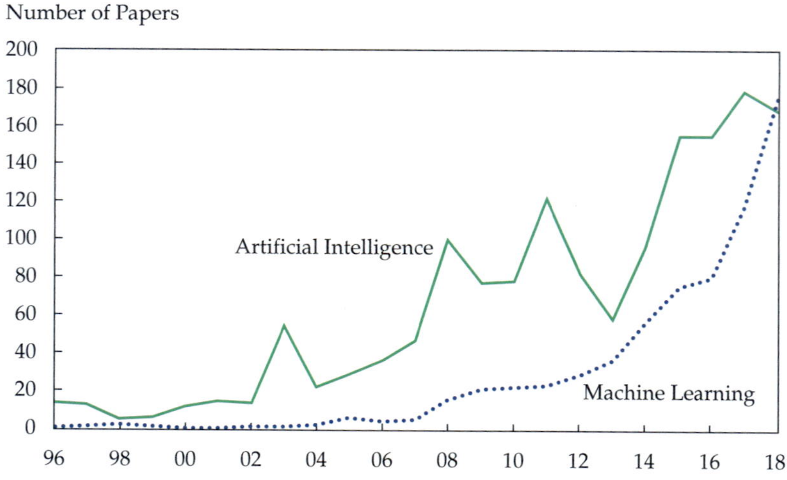

Notes: The figure presents the number of published papers with specific keywords by year, as reported by the Scopus database. The sample starts in 1996, ends in 2018, and includes papers having either "artificial intelligence" or "machine learning" in their abstract, title, or keyword section.

Second, the volume and breadth of data that can be used to train AI models have increased substantially. Lastly, AI algorithms have been improved and become widely accessible, allowing for their use in many cases without the need for expert computer science knowledge. All these factors have contributed to the popularity of AI and ML as research topics in social sciences.

Although AI is a broad field that entails a range of approaches developed over time, the recent interest in AI is almost entirely centered on ML, which is by far the most popular AI approach to date. ML is concerned with using data progressively to adapt the parameters of statistical, probabilistic, and other computing models. It essentially automates one or several stages of information processing. Although an extensive list of techniques can accomplish this automation, most ML applications in asset management, and even in finance more generally, rely on a number of major (classes of) techniques (**Figure 2**). These include artificial neural networks (ANNs), cluster analysis, decision trees and random forests, evolutionary (genetic) algorithms, least absolute shrinkage and selection operator (LASSO), support vector machines (SVMs), and natural language processing (NLP). Appendix A provides a detailed, more technical description of each of these techniques.

The interest of academic research in specific AI techniques has steadily increased in the past two decades, as illustrated by the number of published papers on the subject (**Figure 3**). Some of these techniques, such as evolutionary algorithms or neural networks, were established research topics long before ML gained popularity. On the other hand, SVMs and NLP have gained interest more recently. Neural network, random forest, and NLP techniques have experienced the sharpest increase in their mention in published papers during the past five years. Appendix B provides a more detailed view of the use of AI techniques in finance research based on analyzing all working papers posted on SSRN. The following sections discuss these techniques and their applications in the context of asset management.

Figure 2. Summary of Key AI/ML Techniques

Technique	Description
Artificial Neural Networks	• Nonlinear regression model • Network of connected nodes that loosely model neurons in a brain • Receives a training set of input and desired output data pairs and is able to learn the relationship between them • Can then be used to predict the output of previously unseen inputs • Typical application: Forecasting
Decision Trees and Random Forests	• A decision tree classifies units based on their features • Classification is done by traversing a logical tree from root to leaves, at each branch moving left or right depending on the unit's features; such trees can be interpreted by humans • Constructed automatically based on training set of input and desired output pairs • Random forests simply average the outputs of several decision tree models in order to produce more reliable forecasts • Typical application: Classification and forecasting
Support Vector Machines	• Can be used for classification or regression • Can handle nonlinear relationships by mapping the inputs to a higher-dimensional space • Faster to train than artificial neural networks • Typical application: Forecasting
LASSO	• Ordinary regression model with an additional penalty term that ensures choosing the smallest necessary subset of explanatory variables • Reduces spurious coefficient estimates to zero, which significantly enhances the out-of-sample performance of the model • Typical application: Forecasting
Cluster Analysis	• Clusters data into groups so that the units in each group have similar characteristics • The number of clusters can be defined by the user or determined automatically by the algorithm • Typical application: Asset classification
Evolutionary (Genetic) Algorithms	• Optimization technique capable of searching through large, complex, nonlinear sets of solutions, identifying those that are preferred • Process inspired by natural evolution • Typical application: Variants of portfolio optimization that cannot be solved with classical optimization algorithms
Natural Language Processing	• Range of techniques used to process natural language data (e.g., textual, audio) • Particularly useful for extracting information from textual media (e.g., social media, websites, news articles) • Typical application: Automatic analysis of corporate annual reports and news articles

Note: The figure lists and describes major AI techniques commonly used in asset management.

Figure 3. Number of Published Papers by AI Technique over Time, 1996–2018

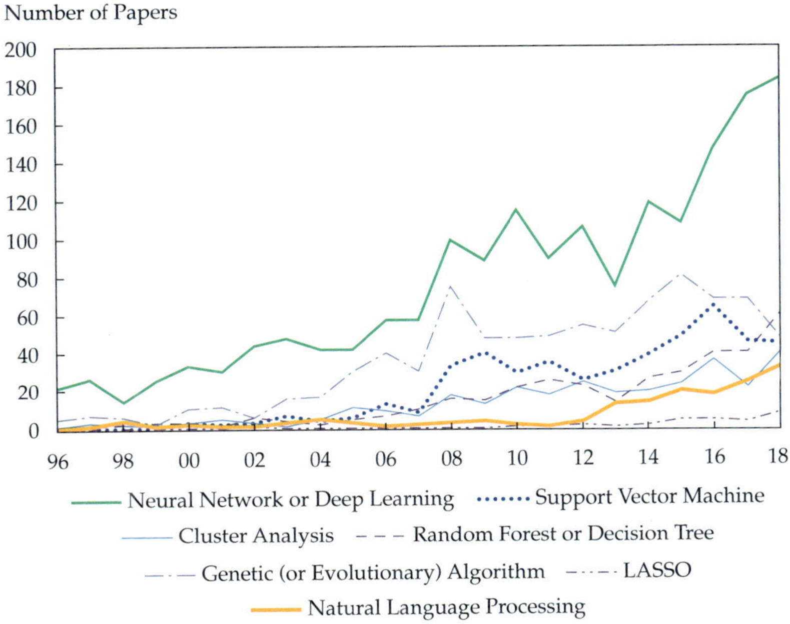

Notes: The figure presents the number of published papers with specific keywords by year. It is based on the number of published papers listed on Scopus starting in 1996 and ending in 2018. The papers have "finance" and/or "asset management" keywords together with at least one of the following keywords: "cluster analysis," "genetic algorithm" or "evolutionary algorithm," "lasso," "natural language processing," "neural network" or "deep learning," "random forest" or "decision tree," and "support vector machine."

3. Portfolio Management

AI techniques can be used to perform sophisticated fundamental analysis, including the use of text analysis, and to optimize asset allocations in financial portfolios. Amid various challenges of conventional portfolio optimization approaches, AI techniques often provide better estimates of returns and covariances than more conventional methods do. These estimates can then be used within traditional portfolio optimization frameworks. Moreover, AI can be used directly for asset allocation decisions to construct portfolios that meet performance targets more closely than portfolios created using traditional methods (**Figure 4**).

3.1. Alpha and Sigma

Fundamental analysis can be considered the cornerstone of portfolio management and can be facilitated significantly by AI (**Table 1**). Arguably the most significant application of AI in fundamental analysis is textual analysis (Das 2014; Kearney and Liu 2014; Fisher, Garnsey, and Hughes 2016).

Figure 4. AI in Portfolio Management

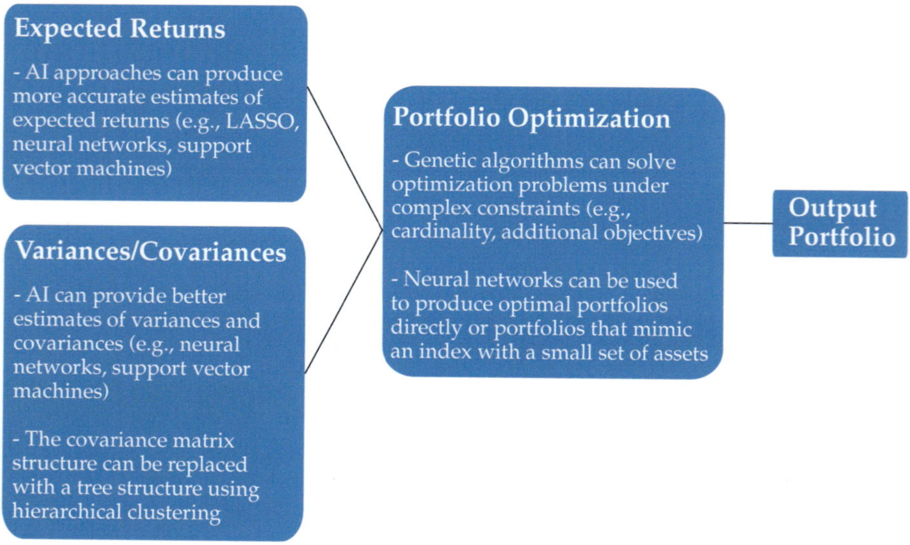

Notes: The figure presents a summary of how AI can be incorporated into portfolio construction. AI approaches can provide the inputs (i.e., expected returns, variance/covariance, and asset views) and use them in asset allocation to meet portfolio managers' targets.

Table 1. AI and Fundamental Analysis

Technique	Study	Sample/Data
ANNs	Atsalakis and Valavanis (2009)	No empirical work; surveys other studies
	Lam (2004)	Financial data for 364 S&P 500 Index companies from 1985 to 1995
	Ballings, Van den Poel, Hespeels, and Gryp (2015)	Financial data for 5,767 listed European firms from 2009 to 2010
Cluster Analysis	Ballings et al. (2015)	Financial data for 5,767 listed European firms from 2009 to 2010
Decision Trees	Ballings et al. (2015)	Financial data for 5,767 listed European firms from 2009 to 2010
	Bryzgalova, Pelger, and Zhu (2019)	Financial data for all US firms available on CRSP from 1964 to 2016
Genetic Algorithms	Hu, K. Liu, Zhang, Su, Ngai, and M. Liu (2015)	No empirical work; surveys other studies
Hybrid/ Ensemble	Li, Huang, Deng, and Zhu (2014)	Stock data for all HKEX-listed firms in year 2001
	Huang (2012)	Financial data for 200 stocks listed on the Taiwan Stock Exchange from 1996 to 2010
LASSO	Feng et al. (2017)	NYSE, AMEX, and NASDAQ stock data from 1976 to 2017
NLP	Leung and Ton (2015)	Stock data for 2,000 firms listed on the Australian Securities Exchange (ASX) from 2003 to 2008
	Sprenger et al. (2014)	400,000 stock-related Twitter messages and S&P 500 stock prices for 2010
	Schumaker and Chen (2006)	9,211 financial news articles and 10,259,042 stock quotes for a five-week period in 2005
SVMs	Han and Chen (2007)	Financial statement data for 251 stocks listed on the Shanghai Stock Exchange and Shenzhen Stock Exchange
	Fan and Palaniswami (2001)	Financial data for stocks listed on the ASX from 1992 to 2000
	Ballings et al. (2015)	Financial data for 5,767 listed European firms from 2009 to 2010

Note: The table presents a list of frequently cited studies that use one or several major AI techniques (hybrid or ensemble approaches) for fundamental analysis.

NLP approaches are capable of extracting economically meaningful information from various sources of text, such as corporate annual reports (Azimi and Agrawal 2019), news articles (Schumaker and Chen 2006; Ke, Kelly, and Xiu 2019), and Twitter posts (Sprenger, Sandner, Tumasjan, and Welpe 2014). Unlike more traditional textual analysis techniques, such as dictionary-based approaches that extract information only from individual words in the text, AI approaches can also interpret context and sentence structure.

LASSO regression can automatically select the factors with the highest explanatory power for future returns from a large set of return-predictive signals documented in the literature (Feng, Giglio, and Xiu 2017; Freyberger, Neuhierl, and Weber 2018). The LASSO framework can also be used to find lead–lag relationships between asset groups or markets. For example, one can investigate which domestic industry or market returns are the most significant predictors of returns among all other markets or industries (Rapach, Strauss, and Zhou 2013; Rapach, Strauss, Tu, and Zhou 2019). More-generalized versions of LASSO regression, known as "elastic nets," complement LASSO's variable selection feature by also ensuring that estimated coefficients are not disproportionately large (e.g., Gu et al. 2020). In addition, AI models can be used to identify stocks expected to outperform or underperform, using a range of economic or firm-level variables. The results of these analyses can then be incorporated into the portfolio optimization process by allocating more (less) weight to assets with high (low) alpha. Beyond using historical data, training AI using actual experts' stock buy or sell recommendations (Bew, Harvey, Ledford, Radnor, and Sinclair 2019; Papaioannou and Giamouridis, forthcoming) has also been successful.

Across AI techniques available for return prediction, ANNs have been found to perform best compared with ordinary least squares regression, elastic nets, LASSO regressions, random forests, and gradient boosted regression trees (Gu et al. 2020). In fact, the out-of-sample predictions of an ANN with three hidden layers were almost 30% more accurate than those generated by a gradient boosted regression tree, which was the second best-performing technique among the six. Note that these results might be highly task- and data-specific. Nevertheless, the success of neural networks in this case is largely attributed to their ability to capture complex nonlinear relationships. In addition, these models stand apart because they are highly versatile and because a large number of functional forms and structures are available that allow neural networks to learn from data more effectively than other techniques. Recent studies have also introduced methods of interpreting neural networks statistically using confidence intervals and by ranking the importance of input variables and interaction effects (Dixon and Polson 2019).

Not surprisingly, neural networks are therefore one of the most popular AI techniques for predicting stock returns (Vui, Sim, Soon, On, Alfred, and Anthony 2013; Abe and Nakayama 2018), company fundamentals (Alberg and Lipton 2017), and returns of other asset classes such as bonds (Bianchi, Büchner, and Tamoni 2019). However, evidence is also available that indicates vector machines can be better at predicting the first two moments of asset returns than ANNs can, provided they are tuned appropriately (Huang, Nakamori, and Wang 2005; Chen, Shih, and Wu 2006; Arrieta-ibarra and Lobato 2015). Consequently, a popular implementation consists of using the average prediction across various AI techniques. This "ensemble" approach has been shown to produce better predictions than any individual AI technique (Rasekhschaffe, Christian, and Jones 2019; Borghi and De Rossi, forthcoming). Recent findings indicate that AI signals generate significant profits in both short and long positions (0.78% abnormal returns per month for a long-only, value-weighted portfolio) and that these profits remain statistically and economically significant even in the post-2001 period, during which a global decay is seen in abnormal returns (Avramov, Cheng, and Metzker 2019).

Modeling and predicting asset prices becomes a particularly challenging exercise when derivatives are involved. As a result, constructing optimal portfolios that include derivatives is difficult, because their prices and payoffs are not well defined and are contingent on other assets. Most conventional derivative pricing approaches rely heavily on theoretical models, such as Black–Scholes, that are based on somewhat restrictive assumptions. This is, again, a realm where AI can play a role. For example, ANNs can be used for pricing and hedging using nonparametric option pricing frameworks that perform better than the Black–Scholes model in terms of delta hedging (Hutchinson, Lo, and Poggio 1994) and forecasting future option prices (Yao, Li, and Tan 2000). Recent studies also extend the deep learning framework to price exotic (Becker, Cheridito, and Jentzen 2019a) and American-style (Becker, Cheridito, and Jentzen 2019b) options.

Lastly, AI can be used for improving estimates of variance–covariance matrices in the Markowitz framework. To illustrate, hierarchical cluster analysis can replace the covariance structure of asset returns with a tree structure (de Prado 2016). This approach uses all the information contained in the covariance matrix but requires fewer estimates and thus leads to more stable and robust portfolio weights. Empirical evidence using simulated return observations suggests that a minimum variance portfolio under this approach has a 31.3% higher Sharpe ratio than that under the classical Markowitz (1952) framework.

Ultimately, the jury is still out as to whether AI implementations are generally superior to more traditional implementations in stock selection, factor investing, or asset allocation. More evidence would be desirable to confirm that the benefits of AI models, including their ability to capture nonlinearities, outweigh the costs and potential data issues, such as collinear variables. The additional evidence will only grow more important because many asset managers have recently started using AI, potentially leading to the superior performance of AI-based investment strategies being arbitraged away in the near future. Moreover, other reasons to be cautious also exist. For example, some research advocating the use of AI in portfolio management has examined only small samples of assets or emerging markets that lack liquidity and efficiency. Another challenging aspect of using AI is selecting relevant variables from the raw data and transforming them into appropriate formats for AI models to function properly, also known as "feature engineering." This constitutes an essential and time-consuming part of alpha research (Rasekhschaffe et al. 2019).

3.2. Portfolio Optimization

A portfolio manager's decision entails allocating funds among a (large) set of assets such that the target portfolio satisfies an objective (e.g., mimicking an index, maximizing the Sharpe ratio), given certain constraints. The mean–variance framework of Markowitz typically offers the theoretical foundation. However, two main challenges arise in practice (Michaud and Michaud 2008; Kolm, Tütüncü, and Fabozzi 2014). First, the optimal asset weights are highly sensitive to estimates of expected returns. Considering that estimates of future expected returns are often uncertain, the optimization exercise can yield unstable weights that perform poorly out of sample. In fact, the noise in return estimates can erode any diversification benefits. For example, DeMiguel, Garlappi, and Uppal (2009) show that an equally weighted portfolio has a higher out-of-sample Sharpe ratio than the optimal Markowitz portfolio and a range of other optimal portfolios.

Second, estimating the variance–covariance matrix, which is at the heart of Markowitz's theory, requires a large time series of data and the assumption of stable correlations between asset returns. Moreover, the matrix becomes unstable when asset correlations increase, which happens at times when diversification is most important and yet more difficult to achieve (de Prado 2016).

AI addresses these challenges in two ways. First, it can produce return and risk estimates that are more accurate than those produced by other methods and that can be used within traditional portfolio construction frameworks. Second, AI techniques can provide alternative portfolio construction approaches to generate more accurate portfolio weights and produce optimized portfolios with better out-of-sample performance than those generated by traditional linear techniques. Although empirical evidence is limited, interest seems to be growing among both academics and practitioners.

In particular, ANNs can be trained to make asset allocation decisions subject to complex constraints that are often not straightforward to integrate into the mean–variance framework. For example, a neural network can select portfolios according to a learning criterion that maximizes returns subject to value-at-risk constraints (Chapados and Bengio 2001). ANNs can also solve complex multi-objective optimization problems. To illustrate, a neural network–based methodology can construct a mean–variance-skewness optimal portfolio in a fast and efficient manner (Yu, Wang, and Lai 2008). Furthermore, ANNs can incorporate views about the future asset performance into the portfolio optimization using a Black and Litterman (1992) framework, generating higher out-of-sample Sharpe ratios than the market portfolio (Zimmermann, Neuneier, and Grothmann 2002).

Another popular AI technique in portfolio construction is evolutionary algorithms that have the flexibility to accommodate more complex asset allocation problems. For example, evolutionary algorithms solve optimization problems under cardinality constraints (restricting the number of assets in the portfolio) and maximum or minimum holding thresholds (Branke, Scheckenbach, Stein, Deb, and Schmeck 2009). Evolutionary algorithms are also able to incorporate additional objectives. For example, one can incorporate model risk (i.e., the risk of failing to produce accurate estimates of asset returns and volatilities as a result of model mis-specifications) into the optimization problem to reduce forecasting error (Skolpadungket, Dahal, and Harnpornchai 2016). Optimal portfolios using this approach have better-realized Sharpe ratios by approximately 10% than those that consider only return and volatility in their objective functions.

The ability of ANNs to capture nonlinear relationships between assets without any prior knowledge about the underlying structure of the data can be useful in synthetic replication—that is, replicating a benchmark portfolio such as an index by holding a fraction of the constituents while minimizing tracking error by matching some of the benchmark's risk factors. For example, ANNs can approximate the Financial Times Stock Exchange (FTSE) 100 Index with only seven stocks (Lowe 1994), resulting in lower transaction costs from portfolio rebalancing as well as reduced portfolio management and monitoring costs. This framework has promising out-of-sample performance and is flexible enough to generate target portfolios with other specified characteristics. For example, one can find the best strategy (i.e., the strategy with the lowest risk or cost) to construct a portfolio that outperforms a specific index by 1% on an annual basis (Heaton, Polson, and Witte 2017).

4. Trading

Algorithms can play a role in all stages of the trading process (Nuti, Mirghaemi, Treleaven, and Yingsaeree 2011). The trading process can be broken down into pre-trade analysis, trade execution, and post-trade analysis (**Figure 5**). Pre-trade analysis entails using data to analyze properties of financial assets with the objective of forecasting not only their future performance but also the risks and costs involved in trading them. Insights from this analysis ultimately lead to the execution of trades. Pre-trade analysis

Figure 5. Algorithmic Trading with AI

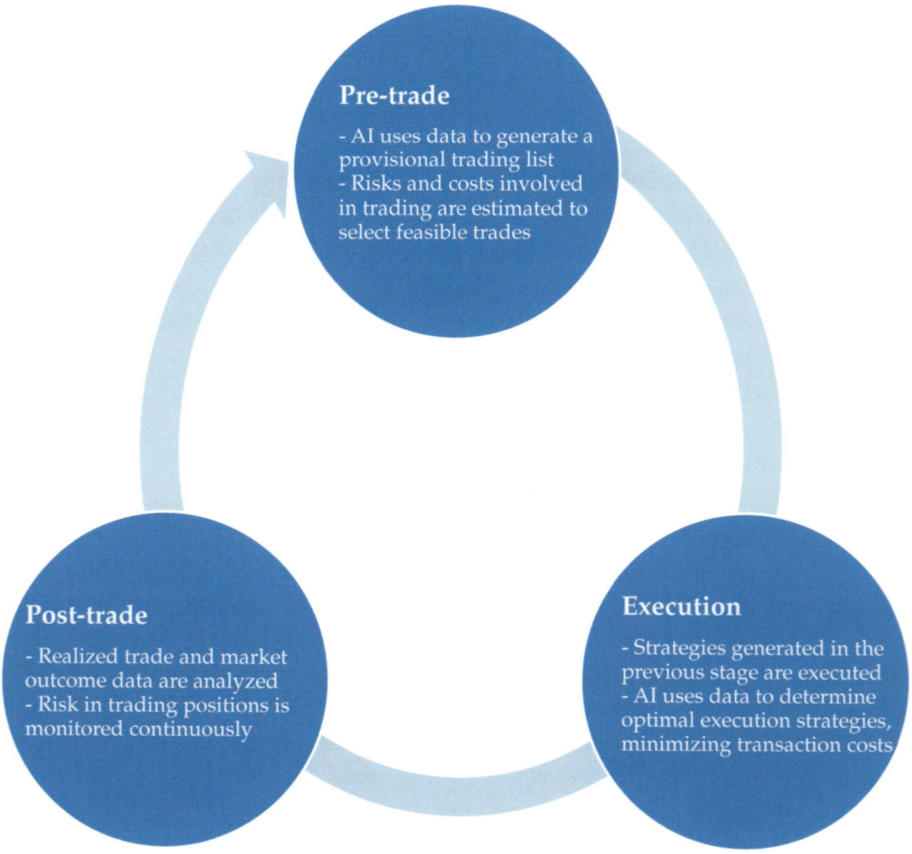

Note: The figure presents the three stages of algorithmic trading and summarizes the applications of AI in each stage.

can be a manual stage, meaning it involves some form of human supervision, given that asset managers might want to consider results from pre-trade analyses together with risk assessments and client preferences. In high-frequency or fully automated systems, however, pre-trade analysis does not involve any human intervention. Trade execution implements trades while ensuring low transaction costs. Actual trading outcomes are evaluated during post-trade analysis to monitor performance and improve the trading system. Post-trade analysis often involves some form of human supervision or overlay. In contrast, pre-trade analysis and trade execution are handled mostly by algorithms because they require timely and complex analyses.

4.1. Algorithmic Trading

AI plays a role in trading by facilitating algorithmic trading—defined as algorithms that automate one or more stages of the trading process. Algorithmic trading has experienced a growing presence in asset management thanks to three recent phenomena (Kirilenko and Lo 2013). First, developments in computing power, data science, and telecommunication have led to structural changes in the way financial markets operate. Computers are now capable of collecting and analyzing large amounts of data and of executing trades in milliseconds without any human intervention. Second, breakthroughs in quantitative finance and ML have provided the necessary tools for computers to conduct insightful financial analysis faster and more efficiently than human beings. Third, the increasing speed, complexity, and scale of financial markets, together with the breadth of new structural products, have made keeping track of markets and making real-time trading decisions difficult if not impossible for humans, whereas complex AI techniques such as ANNs can now be implemented in close to real time (Leshik and Cralle 2011).

Strategies used in algorithmic trading are often based on technical analysis, which uses past stock and market data to predict future asset returns. Although performing fundamental analysis is also possible, algorithmic trades are often of a high frequency, so that analyzing lower-frequency data such as firm fundamentals is typically less effective. In addition, evidence is available that indicates that technical indicators dominate fundamental ones in generating profitable trading signals using AI (Borghi and De Rossi, forthcoming). Therefore, AI-based approaches have established a more active presence in technical analysis (**Table 2**).

The main inputs to traditional forms of technical analysis are past price and trading volume data. Strategies based on prices often model trends, such as momentum or reversal, and cycles using historical data to forecast future returns. On the other hand, volume-based strategies predict future returns

Table 2. AI and Technical Trading Rules

Technique	Study	Sample/Data
ANNs	Dixon, Klabjan, and Bang (2017)	Five-minute mid-prices for 43 CME-listed commodity and foreign exchange futures from 1991 to 2014
	Choudhry, McGroarty, Peng, and Wang (2012)	JPY/USD, DM/USD, and USD/EUR exchange rates from 1998 and 1999
	Gradojevic and Yang (2006)	CAD/USD exchange rates from 1990 to 2000
	Atsalakis and Valavanis (2009)	No empirical work; surveys other studies
	Dunis, Laws, and Sermpinis (2010)	Daily EUR/USD exchange rates from 1999 to 2007
	Fischer and Krauss (2018)	Daily stock data for the constituents of the S&P 500 from 1992 until 2015
Cluster Analysis	Liao and Chou (2013)	30 industrial indices from TAIEX, Shanghai Stock Exchange/Shenzhen Stock Exchange, and the Hang Seng Index from 2008 to 2011
Decision Trees	Booth, Gerding, and McGroarty (2014)	Stock data for 30 firms from the DAX stock index from 2000 to 2013
	Coqueret and Guida (2018)	Financial data for a sample of between 305 and 599 large US firms from 2002 to 2016
Genetic Algorithms	Hu et al. (2015)	No empirical work; surveys other studies
	Allen and Karjalainen (1999)	S&P 500 Index daily prices from 1928 to 1995
	Manahov, Hudson, and Gebka (2014)	One-minute quote data for six major currency pairs from 2012 to 2013
	Berutich, López, Luna, and Quintana (2016)	Stock data for 21 firms listed on the Spanish market from 2000 to 2013
Hybrid/ Ensemble	Cheng, Chen, and Wei (2010)	TAIEX stock index data from 2000 to 2005
	Tan, Quek, and Cheng (2011)	Stock data for more than 20 firms from the US market from 1994 to 2006
	Tsai, Lin, Yen, and Chen (2011)	Stock data for a subset of the Taiwan stock market companies from 2002 to 2006
	Nuij, Milea, Hogenboom, Frasincar, and Kaymak (2014)	Stock data for all FTSE 350 stocks from January to April 2007
	Geva and Zahavi (2014)	Stock data for 72 S&P 500 firms from 2006 to 2007

(continued)

Table 2. AI and Technical Trading Rules *(continued)*

Technique	Study	Sample/Data
LASSO	Chinco, Clark-Joseph, and Ye (2019)	One-minute returns of NYSE stocks from 2005 to 2012
NLP	Renault (2017)	Dataset of stocks with messages published on StockTwits from 2012 to 2016
	Hagenau, Liebmann, and Neumann (2013)	Stock data for a subset of German and British firms from 1997 to 2011

Note: The table presents a list of frequently cited studies that use one or several major AI techniques (hybrid or ensemble approaches) to devise technical trading rules used in algorithmic trading.

based on recent investor trading activity. Modern technical analysis also incorporates information from other sources, including fund flows, investor trades, and textual data from news articles or online sources. AI techniques using NLP can be particularly useful with respect to these new, unstructured sources of data.

4.2. Transaction Cost Analysis

Analyzing transaction costs is an essential part of pre-trade analysis that indicates whether the costs of trading are small enough for a trading signal to generate profits net of implementation costs. Transaction costs have three main components: bid–ask spreads, market impact costs, and trading commissions. Among these three, market impact costs—defined as the adverse effect of a trade on market prices—are the only costs that are not observable before the trade is initiated. Nevertheless, having an estimate of market impact costs is crucial because they represent a significant portion of transaction costs: Market impact absorbs as much as two-thirds of trading gains made by systematic funds (Financial Stability Board 2017).

AI approaches complement traditional market impact models by providing additional insights. The nonparametric structure of AI techniques, together with their ability to capture nonlinear dynamics, are particularly useful for predicting market impact, and various AI techniques have been tested for this purpose. Performance-weighted random forests are found to outperform linear regression, ANNs, and SVMs in predicting the market impact of a market order by 20% out of sample (Booth, Gerding, and McGroarty 2015). On the other hand, SVMs do not seem to perform particularly well when forecasting market impact, whereas ANNs do well if they are properly defined and estimated (Park, Lee, and Son 2016).

Although these nonparametric techniques perform well in estimating market impact, they have two major shortcomings. First, the majority of approaches have no economic intuition for the drivers of price impact. As a result, they are prone to capturing noise rather than relevant information. Second, these techniques cannot distinguish between permanent and temporary market impact, which would require additional variables, including trade direction and liquidity (Farmer, Gerig, Lillo, and Mike 2006). To address these two issues, a parametric approach such as LASSO regression can be used alongside nonparametric techniques. With LASSO regression, the most informative variables capturing information related to the order book and other sources are selected to predict price impact. Empirical evidence indicates that trade sign, market order size, and liquidity based on best limit order prices are the most important variables for forecasting market impact (Zheng, Moulines, and Abergel 2013). A Bayesian network model is another approach for estimating market impact while providing intuition on the main drivers. Unlike most other ML techniques, this approach can also account for variables with data availability issues and model them as latent variables using Bayesian inference. Thanks to this feature, other important variables can be identified (e.g., net order flow imbalance) and added to the model to improve the forecast (Briere, Lehalle, Nefedova, and Raboun 2019).

Another useful application of AI consists of estimating the market impact of trades in assets that lack sufficient (or any) historical trading data, given that using traditional approaches to estimate the market impact costs is almost impossible in this case. A cluster analysis approach can tackle this problem by identifying comparable assets with similar behavior and using their historical data instead. For example, cluster analysis can allocate bonds into clusters based on their duration, maturity, or value outstanding and measure their similarity according to these variables. Within each cluster, the information of other bonds is used for bonds without sufficient data. Bloomberg's liquidity assessment tool notably uses this technique to provide liquidity information for various assets.

4.3. Trade Execution

Executing large trades often involves significant market impact costs. Therefore, such trades are typically broken up into a sequence of smaller orders, which are easier and cheaper to execute. This approach is known as the execution strategy that requires determining the timing and size of smaller orders using some form of execution model. The objective of such models is to minimize transaction costs while completing the transaction within a specified period. Classical modeling approaches for this problem use stochastic control techniques to determine optimal execution strategies (a methodology that goes back to Bertsimas and Lo 1998). Classical models, however, often rely on restrictive assumptions regarding asset price dynamics and the functional form of market impact (Kearns and Nevmyvaka 2013).

In contrast, AI approaches facilitate trade execution modeling by actively learning from real market microstructure data when determining optimal execution strategies. Recent studies advocate reinforcement learning techniques (i.e., algorithms that receive vectors of microstructure and order book variables, such as bid–ask spread, volume imbalances between the buy and sell sides of limit order book, and signed transaction volume) as input and return optimal execution strategies as output (e.g., Nevmyvaka, Feng, and Kearns 2006; Kearns and Nevmyvaka 2013; Hendricks and Wilcox 2014; Kolm and Ritter, forthcoming). The algorithms essentially learn to map each combination of input variables, known as a "state," to trading actions such that transaction costs are minimized (Kearns and Nevmyvaka 2013).

The advantage of AI-based approaches is that they rely on data rather than normative assumptions to determine market impact costs, price movements, and liquidity. They therefore have the flexibility to adapt as market conditions change and new data become available. These models are often difficult to train and understand, however, especially for large portfolios that benefit the most from a reduction in transaction costs. In addition, systematic execution strategies run the risk of cascading into a systemic event affecting the whole market. A famous precedent for this phenomenon is the so-called flash crash of 2010 (Kirilenko, Kyle, Samadi, and Tuzun 2017).

5. Portfolio Risk Management

AI also has applications in risk management, with regard to both market risk and credit risk (Financial Stability Board 2017; Aziz and Dowling 2019). Market risk refers to the likelihood of loss resulting from aggregate market fluctuation, and credit (or counterparty) risk is the risk of a counterparty not fulfilling its contractual obligations, which results in a loss in value (**Figure 6**). Although AI has broader uses in risk management, these two categories are the most important in asset management.

5.1. Market Risk

Market risk analysis involves modeling, assessing, and forecasting risk factors that affect the investment portfolio. AI can play a role in this area in three ways: (1) making use of qualitative data for risk modeling, (2) validating and

Figure 6. AI Applications in Risk Management

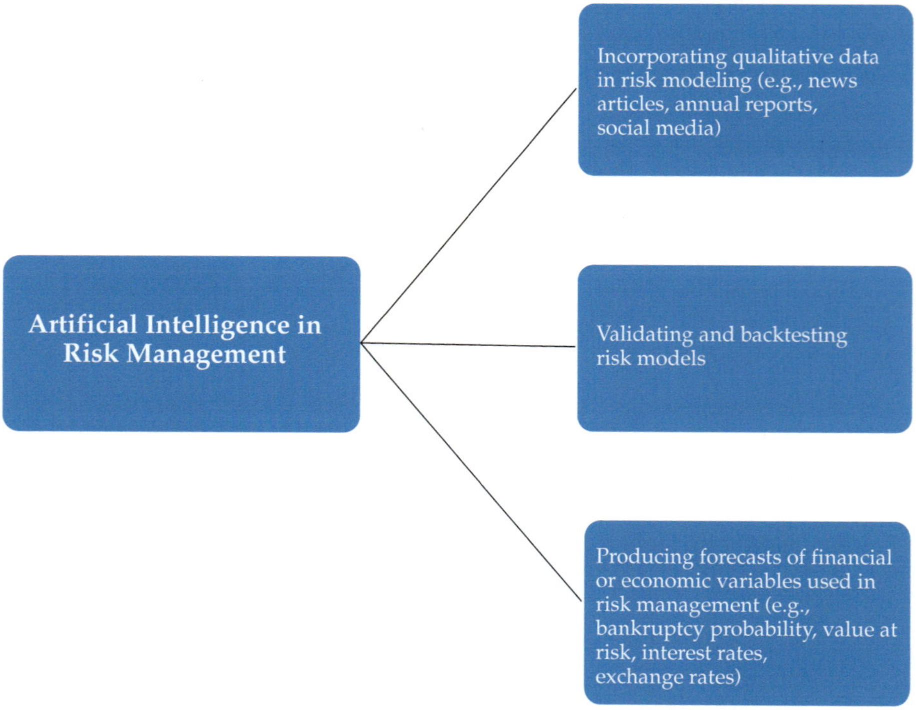

Note: The figure presents a summary of three areas in which AI can play a role in risk management.

backtesting risk models, and (3) producing more accurate forecasts of aggregate financial or economic variables (Figure 6).

One area of application for AI in market risk management relates to extracting information from textual or image data sources. Textual data sources, including news articles, online posts, financial contracts, central bank minutes and statements, and social media, can contain valuable information for managing market risk (Groth and Muntermann 2011). Satellite images are analyzed to predict sales at supermarkets or future crop harvests (Katona, Painter, Patatoukas, and Zeng 2018). The information provided by these sources is, in many cases, not captured by other quantitative variables. For example, AI approaches that use textual information have been shown to generate better predictions of market crashes (Manela and Moreira 2017), interest rates (Hong and Han 2002), and other major macroeconomic outcomes (Cong, Liang, and Zhang 2019) than those using information captured by other data sources. These approaches can also extract information from corporate disclosures with the aim of determining firms' systematic risk profiles (e.g., Groth and Muntermann 2011; Bao and Datta 2014; Cong et al. 2019). All these applications have triggered an interest among central banks in incorporating methods of AI-based text mining in macroprudential analyses (Bholat, Hansen, Santos, and Schonhardt-Bailey 2015). To date, empirical implementations and evidence in this area are scarce.

AI can also help risk managers validate and backtest risk models (Financial Stability Board 2017). Regulators and financial supervisory institutions emphasize this important part of model risk management (Board of Governors of the Federal Reserve System 2011). Unsupervised AI approaches can detect anomalies in risk model output by evaluating all projections generated by the model and automatically identifying any irregularities. Risk managers can also use supervised AI techniques to generate benchmark forecasts as part of model validation practice. Comparing model results and benchmark forecasts will indicate whether the risk model is producing predictions that differ significantly from those generated by AI. A significant disagreement between AI forecasts and standard risk model outputs can highlight potential problems and trigger a more thorough investigation.

Depending on the exposure of the assets in a portfolio to the underlying risk factors, various financial or economic variables can affect its performance. Therefore, modeling future trends in these factors, especially macroeconomic variables, is important (Elliott and Timmermann 2008; Ahmed, Atiya, El Gayar, and El-Shishiny 2010), and ANNs are particularly popular in this context. For example, empirical evidence suggests that variants of ANNs perform significantly better than linear autoregressive approaches in forecasting

47 monthly macroeconomic variables of the G7 economies (Teräsvirta, van Dijk, and Medeiros 2005). Using ANNs entails the risk of producing implausible forecasts at long horizons, however. Nonetheless, ANNs have been particularly successful in forecasting interest rates (e.g., Kim and Noh 1997; Oh and Han 2000) and exchange rates (e.g., Kaashoek and van Dijk 2002; Majhi, Panda, and Sahoo 2009).

ANNs can also be used to devise systematic risk factors. These models can capture nonlinearities and interactions of covariates, including firm characteristics and macroeconomic variables (e.g., Bryzgalova et al. 2019, Chen, Pelger, and Zhu 2020; Gu, Kelly, and Xiu 2019; Feng, Polson, and Xu 2020). Such factors can better account for risk premia and distinguish between nondiversifiable and diversifiable (idiosyncratic) risk than conventional linear factors can. LASSO regressions can also be useful in determining systematic factor structures. These models are able to select the most relevant systematic risk factors from a subset of factors or market indices (Giamouridis and Paterlini 2010).

AI techniques can also predict market volatility and financial crises, especially ANNs and SVMs, whose ability to capture nonlinear dynamics gives them an advantage over traditional generalized autoregressive conditional heteroskedasticity (GARCH) models. ANNs can predict market volatility either directly (Hamid and Iqbal 2004) or in combination with a variant of GARCH (Donaldson and Kamstra 1997; Fernandes, Medeiros, and Scharth 2014). Some researchers, however, found SVMs to be superior to ANNs in this context (Chen, Hardle, and Jeong 2009). In addition to volatility modeling, ANNs and SVMs are used to predict financial crises. Models performing this forecasting task are often referred to as early warning systems. Almost all major financial institutions use a form of early warning system to monitor systemic risk. ANNs and SVMs have been shown to predict currency crises (e.g., Lin, Khan, Chang, and Wang 2008; Sevim, Oztekin, Bali, Gumus, and Guresen 2014), banking crises (e.g., Celik and Karatepe 2007; Ristolainen 2018), and recessions generally (e.g., Yu, Wang, Lai, and Wen 2010; Ahn, Oh, T.Y. Kim, and D.H. Kim 2011; Gogas, Papadimitriou, Matthaiou, and Chrysanthidou 2015) with reasonable accuracy. Nevertheless, crises are rare financial events, so in the absence of a sufficient number of such events in the sample, one could question the ability of AI models to accurately predict future crises.

5.2. Credit Risk

The objective of credit risk management is to ensure that the failure of any counterparty to meet its obligations does not have a negative effect on the portfolio beyond specific limits. Asset managers need to monitor the credit risk of the entire portfolio as well as of individual positions and transactions. This practice involves modeling the solvency risk associated with institutions issuing financial products, including equities, bonds, swaps, and options. An extensive range of approaches exists for modeling solvency or bankruptcy risk. Multivariate discriminant analysis, logit, and probit models are among the most common traditional methods used (Bellovary, Giacomino, and Akers 2007).

Credit risk modeling is one of the first areas of finance to consider the application of AI techniques. The two most widely used techniques are ANNs and SVMs. In fact, ANNs have become mainstream bankruptcy modeling techniques since the early 1990s (Tam 1991). The popularity of ANNs stems largely from their higher success in forecasting bankruptcy and determining credit ratings compared with traditional techniques (e.g., Zhang, Hu, Patuwo, and Indro 1999; Tsai and Wu 2008). More-recent studies, however, advocate the use of SVMs (e.g., Auria and Moro 2008; Ribeiro, Silva, Chen, Vieira, and das Neves 2012) because they yield slightly more accurate bankruptcy forecasts than ANNs do (Huang, H. Chen, Hsu, W.-H. Chen, and Wu 2004). Moreover, SVMs are less likely to face some of the issues common with ANNs, such as overfitting. ANNs and SVMs also perform particularly well when estimating loss given default (defined as the economic loss when default occurs), which the Basel II Accord requires financial institutions to model in addition to the default probability for regulatory capital monitoring purposes (Loterman, Brown, Martens, Mues, and Baesens 2012).

Beyond SVMs and ANNs, a wide range of other AI approaches—including genetic algorithms (Varetto 1998)—can be used for credit risk modeling (Kumar and Ravi 2007; Peña, Martinez, and Abudu 2011). Because each of the modeling techniques has its own specific advantages and disadvantages, an ensemble technique that uses various approaches separately and then combines the resulting predictions should be considered for achieving the best performance (Verikas, Kalsyte, Bacauskiene, and Gelzinis 2010).

6. Robo-Advisors

Robo-advisors are computer programs that provide customized advice to assist individual investors in investment activities. These programs have gained significant attention recently because of their success in reducing barriers to entry for retail investors. Academic interest in researching how to enhance robo-advisors using AI is growing (**Figure 7**). The primary focus is on devising algorithms known as recommender systems that produce optimal portfolios catered to investors' risk appetites (e.g., Xue, Q. Liu, Li, X. Liu, Ye, Wang, and Yin 2018). However, robo-advising can integrate all types of AI

Figure 7. Robo-Advising with AI

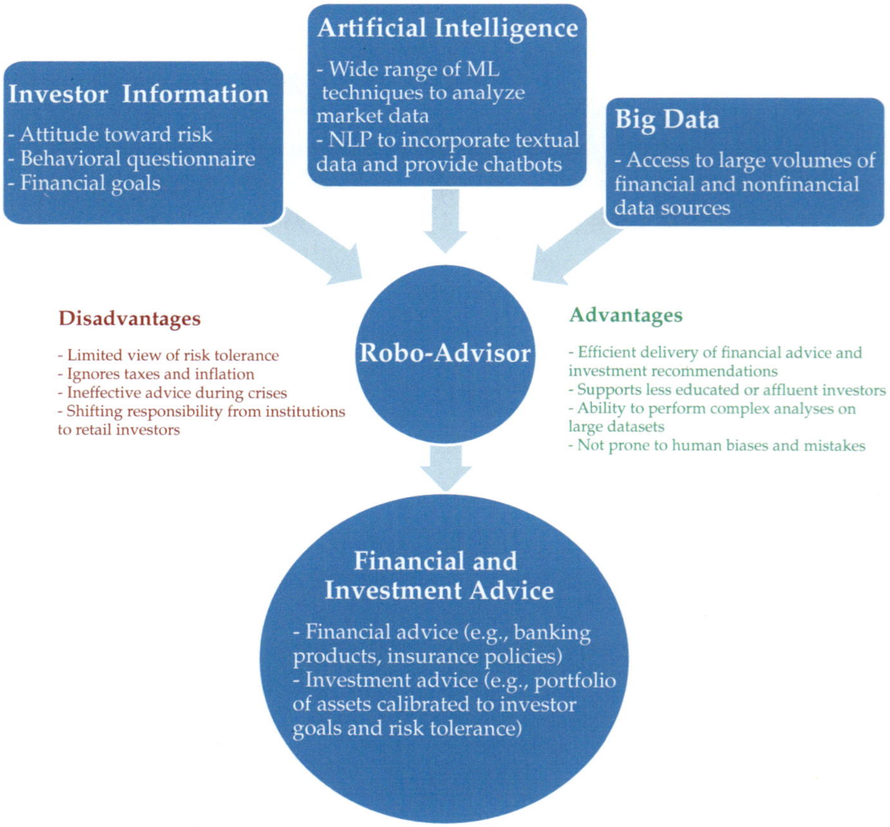

Note: The figure illustrates the structure of robo-advisor systems that incorporate AI and summarizes the advantages and disadvantages of these systems.

applications into portfolio management, trading, and portfolio risk management. By building on the success of AI in these fields, robo-advisors can not only produce portfolios with better out-of-sample performance for investors but also rebalance portfolios, automatically managing the portfolio's risks and minimizing transaction costs. Because robo-advising is less expensive than working with a human advisor and can be performed through a simplified interface, investing via a robo-advisor is ultimately both more beneficial and more accessible for retail investors.

Robo-advisors are also less prone to behavioral biases, mistakes, and illegal practices. In fact, robo-advising has been shown to appeal most to investors who fear being victims of investment fraud (Brenner and Meyll 2019). More sophisticated institutional investors can benefit from robo-advisors' ability to efficiently process a wide range of financial data. Although reducing behavioral biases when making investment decisions is beneficial to all types of investors (D'Acunto, Prabhala, and Rossi 2017), less sophisticated investors particularly benefit from robo-advice in terms of enhancing portfolio performance, increasing diversification, and reducing volatility. At the same time, because robo-advisors have trade execution services integrated into them, they often encourage investors to trade more. This increased trading can be both a benefit, in terms of encouraging investors to rebalance positions more often, and a pitfall, because it can lead to excessive trading that benefits robo-advising systems through commissions at the expense of investors. To be able to use robo-advisors and benefit from their advantages, an investor needs a certain minimum level of technological understanding and financial sophistication.

Not all robo-advisors necessarily use new, sophisticated methods. An analysis of 219 international robo-advisors shows that Markowitz's portfolio theory is the most prevalent approach, although some systems do not disclose their techniques (Beketov, Lehmann, and Wittke 2018). More-sophisticated robo-advisors rely on proprietary algorithms and do not divulge the details of their approach to analyzing portfolios and making recommendations. Nevertheless, an examination of the industry indicates that the most successful robo-advisors rely heavily on AI to conduct investment and trading analyses (Sabharwal 2018). After all, robo-advising and fintech in general derive most of their success from collecting and analyzing data, and AI is an integral part of this process (Dhar and Stein 2017).

7. Artificial Intelligence Risks and Challenges: What Can Go Wrong?

Although many studies of AI in finance highlight the technology's advantages and benefits for various applications, AI users should also be aware of some of its actual or perceived risks and downsides with respect to asset management. These potential negative issues are often related to complexity, opacity, and dependence on data integrity (**Figure 8**).

Understanding and explaining the inferences made by most AI models is difficult, if not impossible. As the complexity of the task or the algorithm grows, opacity can render human supervision ineffective, thereby becoming an even more significant problem. This issue might have repercussions for asset managers in three ways. First, the difficulty in predicting how AI models will respond to major surprises or "black swan" events could lead to systematic crashes. Even in the absence of major events, AI algorithms may make the same errors at the same time, introducing the risk of cascading market crashes. Indeed, the considerable cost of producing AI algorithms has led to most asset management companies using the same tools and algorithms. As a result, AI-driven crashes could be much more likely than other cascading algorithmic crashes we have experienced. Cascading algorithmic crashes are not specific to AI systems and may arise from even simple widespread quantitative approaches, such as value investing. What makes AI different, however, is that its opacity may prevent such risks from being properly modeled and monitored.

Second, AI can make wrong decisions based on incorrect inferences that have captured spurious or irrelevant patterns in the data. For example, ANNs that are trained to pick stocks with high expected returns might select illiquid, distressed stocks (Avramov et al. 2019). Third, attributing investment performance can become more challenging when using AI models. For example, the widely used Barra Risk Factor Analysis, based on linear factor models, might not suit AI-based strategies that capture nonlinear relationships between characteristics and returns. Consequently, in cases of poor fund performance, explaining to investors how and why the investment strategy failed can be difficult, which could undermine investors' trust in the fund or even in the industry. To better understand the behavior of AI models, some people approximate an AI model's prediction behavior by constructing an additional, simpler, and interpretable "surrogate model." Shapley values from game theory can be used to understand how much different feature

Figure 8. AI Areas of Concern

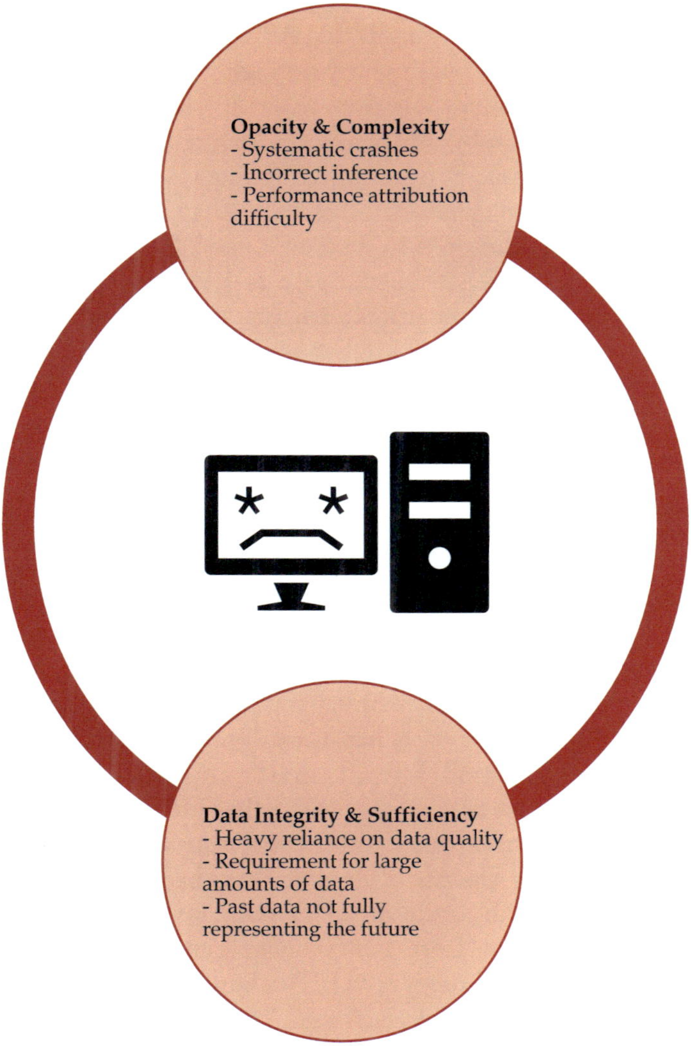

Note: The figure summarizes major potential sources of risk introduced by adopting AI in asset management.

values contribute to a prediction. A good overview on these and many other approaches to explaining AI models can be found in Molnar (2020).

Moreover, the black box character of many AI systems raises the issue of responsibility and makes regulation challenging (Zetzsche, Arner, Buckley, and Tang 2020).

Data quality and sufficiency can be other major sources of concern. Like other empirical models, AI models rely on the integrity and availability of data. Poor data quality can easily trigger what is famously described as "garbage in, garbage out." Data quality and sufficiency become particularly important because AI outputs are often taken at face value. Therefore, identifying data-related issues by evaluating the model outcomes might not be a straightforward exercise. Furthermore, AI models require large amounts of data during the learning phase, often more than are available. This lack of data might lead to improper calibration caused by the input data's poor signal-to-noise ratio, especially in the case of low-frequency financial data with numerous missing observations. Imputation, a preprocessing step in which statistical values are used as substitutes for missing observations (e.g., Kofman and Sharpe 2003), may help, but obviously only to a certain extent. Some argue that past data in general might not fully represent the future. This shortcoming can become particularly prominent when the short time series of available financial data misses certain important extreme events in the past, increasing the likelihood that AI models will fail during a crash or crisis (Patel and Lincoln 2019). As a side effect, AI's growing presence in the investment industry and asset managers' reliance on it for day-to-day tasks might further increase the asset managers' cybersecurity risk (Board of Governors of the Federal Reserve System 2011).

Overall, whether the benefits of AI outweigh the considerable costs of investing in the required software, hardware, human resources, and data systems is not yet clear. After all, limited resources are available for asset managers to develop and test new strategies, so that investment in AI must be considered alongside mutually exclusive, competing research projects. Once the current AI hype has dissipated, investors may become less keen to invest in AI-driven funds, which would make breaking even on investments in AI infrastructure even harder. Thus, asset managers will need to carefully consider both the benefits and costs of AI (Patel and Lincoln 2019; Buchanan 2019), if only not to get cold feet when the next AI winter comes.

8. Conclusion

The use of AI in asset management is an emerging field of interest among both academics and practitioners. AI has vast applications for portfolio management, trading, and portfolio risk management that enable the industry to be more efficient and compliant. It also serves at the heart of new practices and activities, such as algorithmic trading and robo-advising. Nevertheless, AI is still far from replacing humans completely. Indeed, most of its operations within asset management are confined and controlled by some form of human supervision. Consequently, a better way to describe AI is as a collection of techniques that automate or facilitate (often small) parts of the practice of asset management, from the capacity to solve portfolio optimization problems with specific conditions to fully automated algorithmic trading systems.

The success of AI in asset management is linked to its three key, inherent capabilities. First, AI models are objective, highly efficient in conducting repetitive tasks, and able to identify patterns in high dimensional data that may not be perceptible by humans. AI can also analyze data with minimal knowledge of the data's structure or the relation between input and output, including nonlinear relations. This feature is especially useful for forecasting, yielding more accurate estimates because AI does not rely on restrictive assumptions inherent in more traditional methods. Second, AI can extract information from unstructured data sources, such as news articles, online posts, reports, and images. As a result, a tremendous amount of information can be incorporated into financial analysis without manual processing and intervention. Third, AI algorithms, unlike other statistical techniques, are often designed to improve themselves by readjusting in accordance with the data. This ability means that the manual reconfiguration or parameter re-estimation that is essential for traditional models is unnecessary with AI.

Finally, AI's greatest strength—its ability to process data with minimal theoretical knowledge or supervision—can also be its greatest weakness. Indeed, a popular saying asserts that AI will always generate a result, even when one should not exist. This tendency causes problems when data quality is poor, when the task being performed is too complex for humans to monitor or understand, and when cascading systemic failures could occur as a result of several AI algorithms reacting to each other. Asset managers must bear such issues in mind as the role of AI becomes more pervasive and significant.

Appendix A. Basic Artificial Intelligence Concepts and Techniques

A.1. Artificial Intelligence and Machine Learning

A.1.1. Origin and Definition. AI is widely believed to have started at the Dartmouth Summer Research Project on Artificial Intelligence, a workshop organized by John McCarthy in the summer of 1956 at Dartmouth College. Many prominent mathematicians and scientists, including Marvin Minsky and Claude Shannon, attended this six-week brainstorming workshop. The workshop proposal introduced the term "artificial intelligence" and stated the following objectives:

> The study is to proceed on the basis of the conjecture that every aspect of learning or any other feature of intelligence can in principle be so precisely described that a machine can be made to simulate it. An attempt will be made to find how to make machines use language, form abstractions and concepts, solve kinds of problems now reserved for humans, and improve themselves. (McCarthy, Minsky, Rochester, and Shannon 2006, p. 12)

In recent years, the original definition of AI and what it should encompass has evolved. Russell and Norvig (2010) distinguish the following four different dimensions, or schools of thought, that determine the objective of AI.

1. **Acting Humanly:** From this point of view, AI refers to the challenge of creating computers capable of performing tasks in ways that are similar to how humans perform them. An example of this is the Turing Test, proposed by Alan Turing. The test poses a challenge in which a human interrogator presents questions and receives responses from either another human or a machine. The machine passes the test if the interrogator is unable to distinguish the human's answers from the machine's.

2. **Acting Rationally:** This dimension aims to build agents that act rationally, (i.e., that aim to achieve the best outcome or, when uncertainty exists, the best expected outcome).

3. **Thinking Humanly:** This perspective refers to the replication of human thinking processes. The field of cognitive science is a major manifestation of this approach to AI. It uses computer programs and insights from experimental psychology to emulate the human mind.

4. **Thinking Rationally:** Thinking rationally refers to using rules for reaching logical conclusions based on premises assumed to be true.

Until a few decades ago, most research in AI fell into the category of thinking rationally, represented by expert systems. Such systems have large knowledge bases and an inference mechanism that allows the deduction of new knowledge by logically deriving it through rules. For example, knowing that all men are mortal and that Socrates was a man, an expert system could infer that Socrates was mortal. Expert systems were highly popular in the 1970s and 1980s, but the need for building large, complex knowledge bases and the systems' deterministic nature have led to them falling out of favor. The idea to have the machine learn through observations (i.e., ML) eventually turned out to be more applicable in practice, and it is the predominant AI technique behind most modern applications.

Problems studied under ML are of three main types—supervised learning, unsupervised learning, and reinforcement learning (Alpaydin 2010; Murphy 2012)—each of which have common applications. Although many of these techniques have existed for decades, the sudden surge in their popularity and application has resulted from performance improvements thanks to technological progress that has enabled computers to train ML models on a scale that was not possible even a few years ago.

A.1.2. Supervised Learning. Consider the problem of determining the sales price of a house based on a set of attributes, such as interior square footage, geographic location, and number of floors. In supervised learning, an algorithm establishes a mathematical relation between the feature data (square footage, location, and number of floors) and the response data (sales price). Rather than explicitly programming the model, a supervised learning algorithm is given a set of training data. It then adjusts its model so as to minimize the prediction error on the training data. Once the model has been established, it can be used to infer a response from features that have not been observed before. Often the training is iterative (i.e., a relation is first guessed randomly) and subsequently adjusted based on how erroneous the guess was. Over time, increasingly accurate relations are produced until, ideally, a "best" relation is found. Effectively, a machine learns how to relate the feature data to the response data. Because a training set of correctly classified response data is used to guide the learning process, the learning is deemed supervised. Supervised learning is currently the most common learning approach in practice.

Supervised learning has two main applications: classification and regression. Predicting the sales prices of houses is an example of regression, because the response data are quantitative and continuous. In classification, one is interested in determining a response that falls into one of a few categories, such as whether or not a credit card transaction is fraudulent, based on observed features such as the distance of the transaction from the cardholder's residence, the amount of the transaction, and the object purchased.

A.1.3. Unsupervised Learning. Unsupervised learning is used to identify structures in data without access to labels. The most popular example is clustering (i.e., the categorization of data into different groups wherein the elements of each group have similar characteristics). This approach is useful, for example, in marketing, where customers can be separated into different groups, and different marketing strategies can be developed for each group. Other applications are the detection of regularities (e.g., people who buy X also tend to buy Y) and the compression of data.

A.1.4. Reinforcement Learning. The premise of reinforcement learning is that an agent (e.g., a program, a robot, a control system) learns how to act appropriately in an environment based on reward signals it receives in response to its actions. In each iteration, the agent observes the state of the environment, decides how to act, and then receives a reward and information about the next state of the environment. Reinforcement learning is the core technology behind Google's AlphaZero, an algorithm that learned to beat the best human players in the board game Go simply by playing against itself many times. These algorithms can also be used in finance to solve dynamic optimization problems, including portfolio optimization and trading in the presence of transaction costs (Kolm and Ritter, forthcoming).

A.2. Overview of Common Artificial Intelligence Techniques

Several AI techniques are widely used in asset management. These include ANNs, cluster analysis, decision trees, evolutionary (genetic) algorithms, LASSO regression, SVMs, and NLP. This section briefly characterizes these techniques, discusses their strengths and weaknesses, and notes their areas of application (**Table A.1**).

A.2.1. Least Absolute Shrinkage and Selection Operator Regression. Linear regression is a common and relatively simple way to fit a model to data to make predictions or to estimate missing values. It seeks to find the coefficients of explanatory (or predictor) variables that contribute to the value of the dependent (or predicted) variable. To find the best model, the most common approach is to minimize the sum of squared errors, which are the difference between observed values and the values predicted by the model. As model complexity increases with the number of regressors,

Table A.1. Summary of AI Techniques

Technique	Strengths	Weaknesses	Areas of Application
ANNs	— Complex and nonlinear relationships — Incremental and transfer learning — Can generalize well	— Data and computationally intensive — Predictions not explainable — Possible overfitting	— Image processing and recognition — Speech recognition and synthesis — Forecasting
Cluster Analysis	— Labels unnecessary — Helps to understand data	— Clusters may be intertwined — May require cluster count — Choosing attributes can be difficult	— Data analysis — Anomaly detection — Recommendations
Decision Trees	— Classifications are explainable — Complex and nonlinear relationships	— Possible overfitting — Complex trees possible — Poor at predicting continuous variables	— Decision making — Classification
Evolutionary (Genetic) Algorithms	— Ability to handle high-dimensional spaces — Finds novel solutions	— Varies on initial conditions — Computationally intensive	— Parameter optimization — Portfolio optimization
LASSO Regressions	— Identify most relevant features — Flexible and fairly simple — Sparse solutions	— Model can be unstable and hard to interpret — Perform poorly when independent variables are correlated	— Forecasting and robust regression analysis
NLP	— Analyzes and generates text and speech — Finds information in large textual datasets	— Currently primitive and unable to fully understand text	— Search engines and news filtering — Text classification and summarization
SVMs	— Structure of data can be unknown — Can generalize with less overfitting risk	— Difficult to interpret — Kernel difficult to choose for nonlinear classification	— Classification — Regression

Notes: The table summarizes the key characteristics of major AI techniques and the branch of textual analysis approaches known as NLP. For each technique, the table details the key strengths, weaknesses, and areas of application.

however, the variability of predictions can also increase. Furthermore, with too many parameters, the model can overfit to the data, modeling noise rather than the underlying trend and leading to poor generalization to unseen data. The LASSO method (Tibshirani 1996; James, Witten, Hastie, and Tibshirani 2017) improves over standard linear or nonlinear models by additionally penalizing model complexity. By aiming to set some of the model's parameters to zero, LASSO regression automatically identifies the most relevant data features.

A.2.2. Artificial Neural Networks and Deep Learning. ANNs are inspired by biological brains (Aggarwal 2018; Haykin 2009). Similar to what occurs in biological neurons, in each node of an ANN, input signals are aggregated and processed, and the result is forwarded to other nodes. ANNs are often arranged in feedforward layers (**Figure A.1**), with input data applied to an input layer and further processed by a number of hidden layers before arriving at an output layer. ANNs with many hidden layers are called "deep neural networks." ANNs are trained by altering the weights of the connections so that the errors between the predicted and desired data labels are minimized. Once trained, the ANN can be used to predict the output of previously unseen input data.

Figure A.1. Feedforward ANN

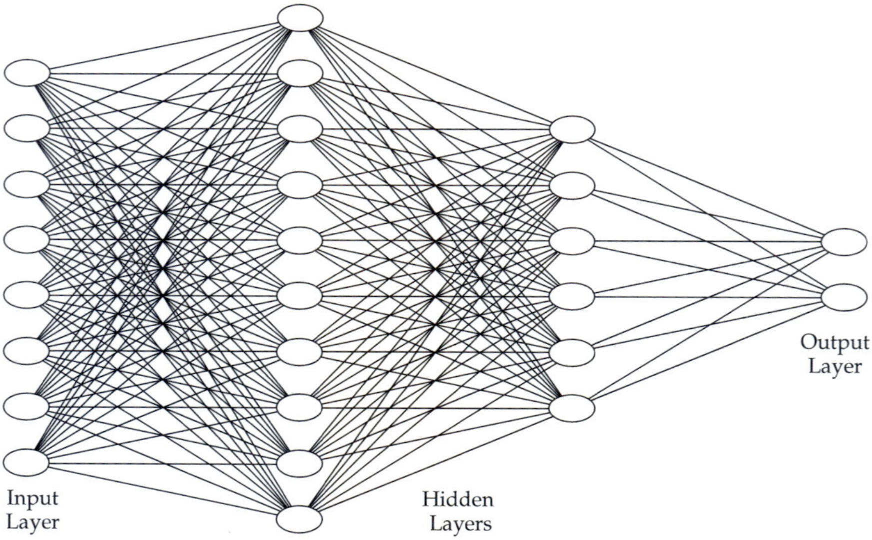

Note: The figure illustrates a fully connected feedforward neural network. Output and input variables are linked through several layers of interconnected nodes.

A fundamental concern among AI practitioners and researchers is the interpretability of trained ANNs. Presently, determining how a given neural network settles on its predictions is not easy. For some fields, this is not an issue. In others, however, such as medical data analysis, doctors are reluctant to use a neural network without a complete understanding of the mechanisms by which the network arrives at a prediction. ANNs also require fairly large datasets to train properly, which may not be available for all assets or markets.

A.2.3. Decision Trees and Random Forests. A decision tree sequentially splits a dataset into increasingly small subsets typically based on a single feature value. For the leaf nodes, the predicted class is determined (**Figure A.2**). Besides classification, decision trees can also be used for piecewise linear regression. Decision trees are a form of supervised learning, and the tree is constructed to replicate the labels in the training data as best as possible.

A random forest (Breiman 2001) is an ensemble of classification and regression methods that consists of many decision trees. Each decision tree makes predictions and contributes to the random forest's predictions via an averaging procedure. The assumption is that many decision tree models, each with a slightly different perspective, make better predictions than a single

Figure A.2. Decision Tree Classifier

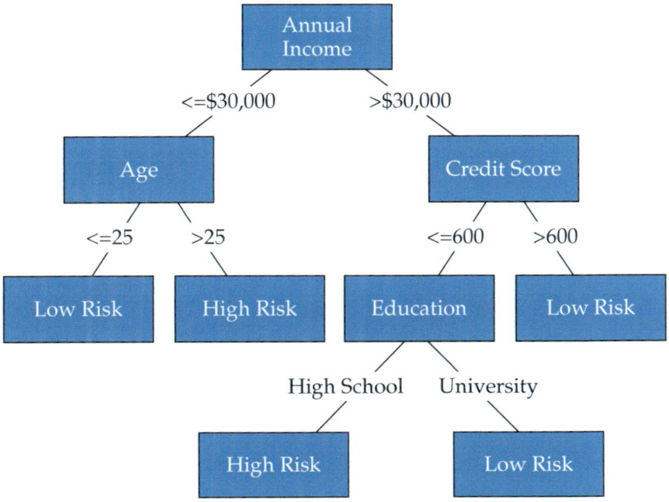

Note: Shown is a decision tree to classify credit applications into low and high risk. Starting from the top, applications move down the tree based on their characteristics. For example, an application of someone with an income less than or equal to $30,000 annually and who is more than 25 years old would be classified as high risk.

decision tree. Individual trees are generated from a distinct sampling of the training set while using a random subset of the attributes for nodes. Consensus voting on tree classifications determines the prediction (**Figure A.3**). A key advantage decision trees have over other AI techniques, such as ANNs, is that the rules they use to classify data are human readable, and thus the reasons that lead to a particular classification can be easily traced.

A.2.4. Support Vector Machines. SVMs are supervised algorithms that are typically used for classification (Vapnik 2000; James et al. 2017). These algorithms learn boundaries that partition the feature space into two or more classes. Once defined, the boundaries can be used to classify new data. SVMs are powerful, accurate tools for both classification and regression, and they are resistant to overfitting their training data. They are computationally intensive, however, and thus do not scale well to large datasets.

Figure A.4, Panel A, presents an example of linearly separable training data. The separation of the data into two classes is defined by the solid line, which has been chosen to maximize its distance from the nearest data point in each class (indicated by the dashed lines). In this example, the SVM has learned the linear boundary that most effectively separates the data. In practice, training data are not always distributed in a way that permits separation by a linear boundary. In such instances, kernel methods are used to find more complex separation boundaries (Cortes and Vapnik 1995). Figure A.4,

Figure A.3. Random Forest Voting Scheme for Classification

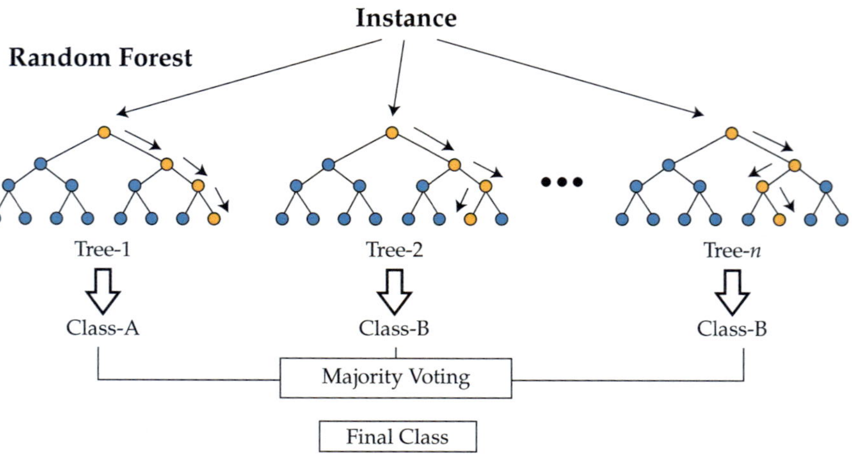

Note: The figure illustrates a random forest voting scheme that makes a prediction. The random forest combines the output of n decision trees and yields a final output that the majority of trees agree on.

Figure A.4. SVM Examples

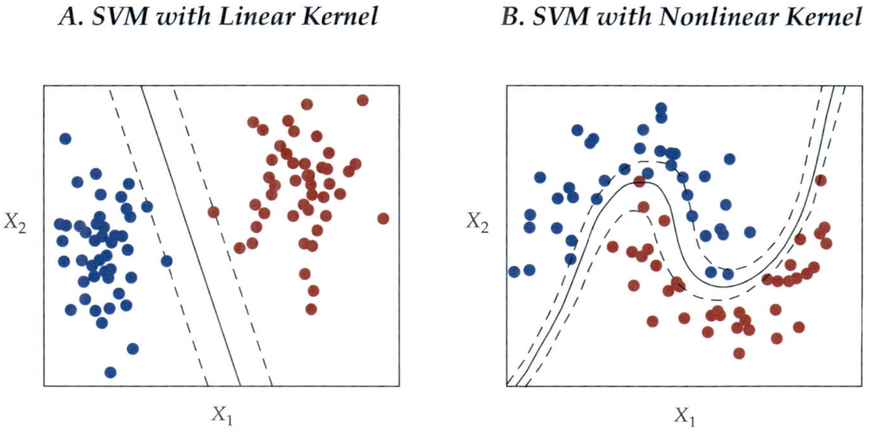

Notes: The figure illustrates an example of using an SVM to separate data into two groups. The dashed lines are the support vectors. SVMs often transform data by adding an additional dimension, making the classification of the data points easier. These transformations are called kernels. Panel A uses a linear kernel, and Panel B uses a nonlinear one.

Panel B, shows a nonlinear boundary learned by an SVM with the radial basis function kernel.

A.2.5. Cluster Analysis. Cluster analysis is an unsupervised learning technique that seeks to partition a dataset into groups or clusters (Tan, Steinbach, Karpatne, and Kumar 2018; Aggarwal and Reddy 2014). Once the clusters are identified and labeled, the model can be used to classify new data. The same data may yield many different possible sets of clusters, depending on the number of clusters desired, how the data are distributed, and the clustering algorithm. Applications in asset management include cluster analysis of markets, companies, financial instruments, time series, and documents.

The most popular clustering algorithm is K-means clustering, which requires the user to specify the desired number of clusters, K. The method starts by randomly choosing some cluster centroids and allocating each data point to the closest centroid. It subsequently alternates between moving each centroid to the center of its data cluster and reassigning the data points.

A.2.6. Evolutionary (Genetic) Algorithms. An evolutionary algorithm (often also called a genetic algorithm) is an optimization algorithm based on Darwin's theory of evolution by natural selection (Eiben and Smith 2015; Simon 2013). Its basic operations are depicted in **Figure A.5**. The evolutionary algorithm starts with an initial population of candidate solutions, usually

Figure A.5. Iteration of an Evolutionary Algorithm

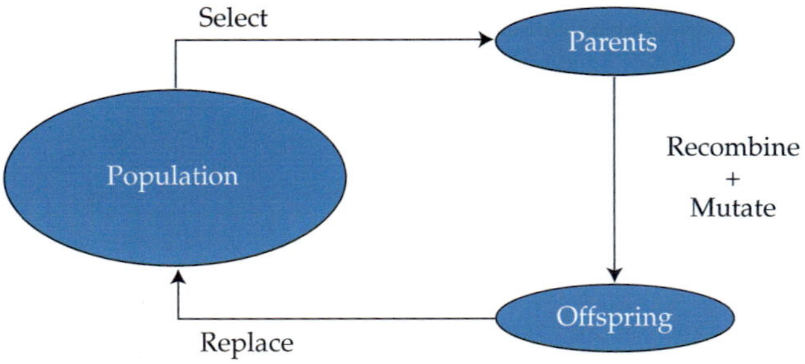

Note: Illustrated is one iteration of an evolutionary algorithm: Better-performing solutions are selected as parents, then used to create new solutions (offspring) by means of recombination and mutation, and finally, the offspring replaces solutions in the population.

generated randomly. In each iteration, new candidate solutions are created by selecting a pair of better performing solutions in the population, merging the information from these two solutions into one (recombination), and introducing small random perturbations (mutation). The new solutions replace older, worse-performing solutions in the population. Via an iterative process of varying previously found well-performing solutions and selectively keeping better ones, increasingly better solutions are found over time.

Because evolutionary algorithms do not require a mathematical formulation of the problem and do not make assumptions such as convexity or linearity about the objective function, they can also be applied to complex problems in which other optimization algorithms fail. For example, evolutionary algorithms have been used to solve mean–variance portfolio selection problems under cardinality constraints (restricting the number of assets in the portfolio).

A.2.7. Natural Language Processing. NLP is a group of computational methods that can process or generate human natural language such as text or speech (Manning and Schütze 1999; Mitkov 2014). These methods include voice recognition, which converts spoken language to text; speech generation, which converts text to speech; natural language understanding, which extracts meaning from spoken or written text; and natural language generation, which produces natural language data from other data sources.

Owing to the ubiquity of social media and the countless natural language samples it provides, the amount of literature on NLP has increased exponentially in recent years (Xing, Cambria, and Welsch 2018). Various SVMs and neural network architectures, such as deep learning or recurrent networks, are frequently used in NLP.

In finance, much attention is focused on natural language financial forecasting, which extracts information such as sentiment from financial news or social media data and incorporates it into models that predict the movement of financial data. Most of the literature applies NLP to stock and foreign exchange rate prediction because of the accessibility of information for these markets.

A.2.8. Comparisons of AI Techniques. AI algorithms and techniques differ by the types of data on which they best operate; the kinds of predictions they can make; the means by which they learn to fit their data; the computational power required for training, testing, and deployment; and the ease with which they can be scaled.

Data may be low dimensional, as in the case of housing price data that depend on fewer than a dozen features, or high dimensional, as in the case of an image consisting of millions of pixels that have values independent from all others. Data that reside in just a few dimensions allow using simpler techniques (e.g., LASSO, K-means clustering, K-nearest neighbors) for classification or regression. On the other hand, data that live in higher dimensions suffer from the curse of dimensionality: The more dimensions the machine learning problem has, the more samples are required to make meaningful predictions, and the more computationally intensive analyzing and modeling the data become. Autoencoder neural networks are an example of an algorithm that can project high-dimensional data into low dimensions, so that the data can be modeled and predicted more effectively.

If the data are labeled, a wide variety of supervised learning algorithms can be used to learn a good mapping from input to predicted output. If data are unlabeled, unsupervised learning techniques, such as cluster analysis, can be used to identify patterns in the data.

Some algorithms are versatile, whereas others are relatively restricted. For instance, K-means clustering is an algorithm designed to partition data into K subsets in an unsupervised fashion only. Neural networks, on the other hand, are more broadly applicable. They can be used for unsupervised and supervised learning, classification, and regression, and they can be applied to images, text, and time series.

The interpretability of a mathematical model varies widely. Linear regression models, logistic regression models, decision trees, and K-nearest neighbor classifiers are examples of algorithms with readily understood learned behavior. In contrast, a precise statistical description of the learning and prediction decisions of neural networks is still an unresolved problem.

Some algorithms are difficult to deploy on large datasets as a result of their computational complexity. Specialized hardware or graphic cards may speed up computations, such as for neural networks. Note that although training is sometimes very time consuming, deploying a trained model for predictions on unseen data is usually fast.

The business logic of asset management determines the structure of datasets and the type of predictions to be obtained. Consequently, the business needs ultimately determine the choice of AI algorithm.

Appendix B. Trends and Patterns in Finance Research Using AI

Developments in academic research related to AI can be analyzed by studying trends and patterns in working papers in finance that use AI techniques. To capture the most recent trends and those related to the area of finance, we downloaded all working papers that have AI-related keywords in their title, abstract, or listed keywords and that have been posted in the Financial Economics Network (FEN) on the Social Sciences Research Network (SSRN) between 1996 and 2018. The primary keywords are "artificial intelligence," "machine learning," "cluster analysis," "genetic algorithm" or "evolutionary algorithm," "lasso," "natural language processing," "neural network" or "deep learning," "random forest" or "decision tree," and "support vector machine."

On SSRN, 1,814 working papers include at least one of our keywords. By far the most popular AI-related keyword, "machine learning" appears in 29% of all papers in our sample. Among AI techniques, "neural network" (or "deep learning"), with 38% of the papers, and "cluster analysis," with 16%, are the two most popular keywords (Panel A of **Figure B.1**). Download numbers magnify the relative popularity of neural networks even further, considering that papers with "neural network"/"deep learning" keywords account for almost half of the total downloads of all papers related to the AI techniques (Panel B of Figure B.1). "Random forest" (or "decision tree"), with only 16%, has the second highest proportion of downloads. Finally, "natural language processing" is associated with only 4% of the papers and 3% of downloads, the lowest among all techniques.

Interestingly, no working papers with a "machine learning" keyword appear until 2003. Because the terms "machine learning" and "artificial intelligence" have gained popularity more recently, we sum the number of papers for all AI-related keywords. In 1996, no working paper with any AI-related keyword was uploaded to SSRN. Significant growth has occurred since, however, with 410 papers posted in 2018. The total number of papers on FEN also increased during the same period, but to a much smaller degree: Papers with AI-related keywords accounted for 3% of all papers in 2018.

Among the AI techniques, the popularity of "neural network" is consistent over the years. "Lasso" and "support vector machine" techniques seem to have gained popularity more recently, however. The same applies to "natural

Figure B.1. Number and Downloads of Finance Papers Using AI, 1996–2018

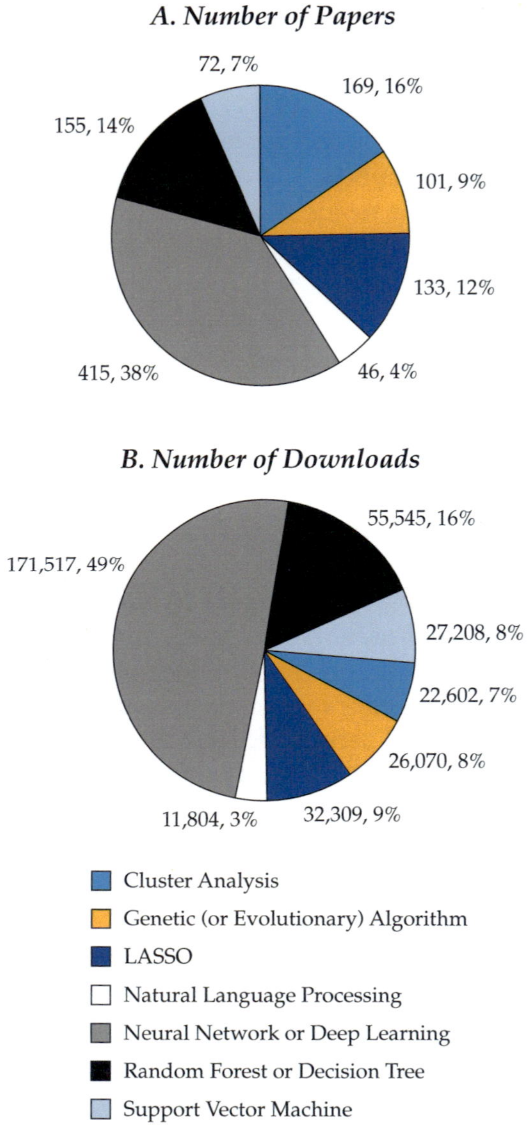

Notes: The figure shows the number of papers (Panel A) and downloads (Panel B) associated with various AI techniques for the sample of SSRN FEN working papers. The sample includes papers having one of the following keywords in their abstract, title, or keyword section: "artificial intelligence," "machine learning," "cluster analysis," "genetic algorithm" or "evolutionary algorithm," "lasso," "natural language processing," "neural network" or "deep learning," "random forest" or "decision tree," and "support vector machine."

language processing": No papers with this keyword appear on SSRN until 2008, but 13 working papers with this keyword were uploaded in 2018.

Among countries, the United States, the United Kingdom, and Germany are the top three producers of papers with AI-related keywords (**Figure B.2**). These three countries account for more than half of all AI papers, followed by Switzerland, India, France, China, and Italy. Not surprisingly, these countries also show high productivity in terms of finance papers generally.

Among institutions, Cornell University, Humboldt University of Berlin, the University of Chicago, Stevens Institute of Technology, and ETH Zurich are the top five contributors to AI research papers (**Table B.1**). A large number of nonacademic institutions are also in the full list, illustrating the interest in conducting research related to this topic in the finance industry and central banks.

Figure B.2. Number of Papers Using AI by Country, 1996–2018

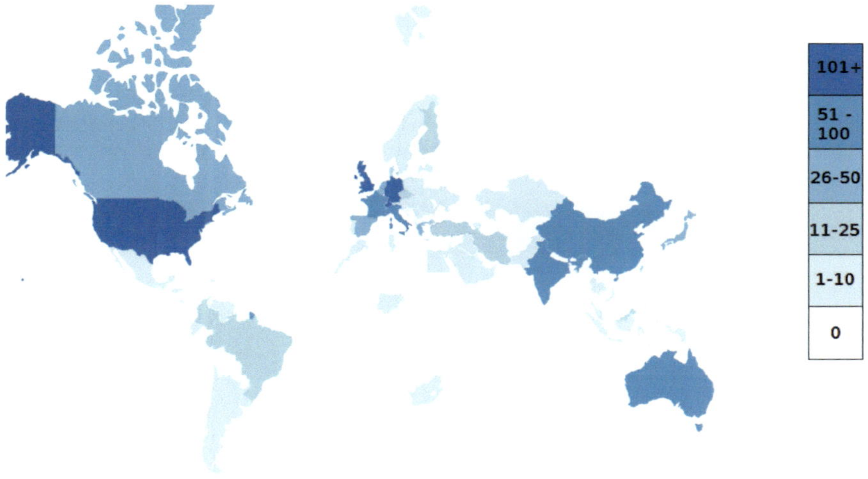

Notes: The figure shows a heat map based on the number of papers with AI-related keywords for each country. A paper belongs to a specific country if at least one of its authors is affiliated with institutions located in that country. The sample includes papers having one of the following keywords in their abstract, title, or keyword section: "artificial intelligence," "machine learning," "cluster analysis," "genetic algorithm" or "evolutionary algorithm," "lasso," "natural language processing," "neural network" or "deep learning," "random forest" or "decision tree," and "support vector machine."

Table B.1. Number of Papers by Institution, 1996–2018

Institution/University	Sum of AI Papers
Independent	75
Affiliation not provided to SSRN	67
Cornell University	64
Humboldt University of Berlin	47
University of Chicago	42
Stevens Institute of Technology	41
ETH Zurich	39
New York University	30
Imperial College London	26
Harvard University	22
University of St. Thomas	21
London School of Economics and Political Science	19
Other Institutions	2,937

Notes: The table presents the number of SSRN FEN working papers by institution. A paper belongs to an institution if at least one of its authors has an affiliation with that institution. The sample includes papers having one of the following keywords in their abstract, title, or keyword section: "artificial intelligence," "machine learning," "cluster analysis," "genetic algorithm" or "evolutionary algorithm," "lasso," "natural language processing," "neural network" or "deep learning," "random forest" or "decision tree," and "support vector machine." Institutions with fewer than 15 papers are combined and reported as "Other Institutions."

References

Abe, Masaya, and Hideki Nakayama. 2018. "Deep Learning for Forecasting Stock Returns in the Cross-Section." In *Advances in Knowledge Discovery and Data Mining*, Part 1, edited by Dinh Phung, Vincent S. Tseng, Geoffrey I. Webb, Bao Ho, Mohadeseh Ganji, and Lida Rashidi, 273–84. Cham, Switzerland: Springer International Publishing.

The authors examine the performance of deep learning for one-month-ahead forecasting of stock returns in the cross-section in the Japanese stock market. Deep neural networks (DNNs) are found to perform better than shallow neural networks and other ML techniques, such as support vector regression (SVR) and random forests. An ensemble of SVR, random forests, and DNN can provide a further small gain in performance.

Aggarwal, Charu C. 2018. *Neural Networks and Deep Learning*. Cham, Switzerland: Springer. https://doi.org/10.1007/978-3-319-94463-0.

This textbook, aimed at graduate students, researchers, and practitioners, is devoted to studying neural networks, or "deep learning," as it became known in ML literature. It starts with background material on neural network design and its relationship to traditional ML algorithms. The rest of the textbook provides a more detailed discussion of the fundamentals of neural networks (common neural architectures, shallow neural networks and DNNs, radial basis function networks, restricted Boltzmann machines) and the recent advances in the field (recurrent and convolutional neural networks, deep reinforcement learning, neural Turing machines, generative adversarial networks).

Aggarwal, Charu C., and Chandan K. Reddy, eds. 2014. *Data Clustering: Algorithms and Applications*. Boca Raton, FL: CRC Press.

Data clustering is partitioning data into multiple groups where each observation shares some characteristics with other data points within its group. Data clustering issues have been studied in different fields, and this book attempts to bridge the gap by uniting the knowledge gained in ML and data mining literature. The first part of the book discusses data clustering methods (probabilistic, distance based, density based, grid based, and spectral clustering, which clusters high-dimensional and big data). The second part is devoted to the application of data clustering in different fields and situations (clustering categorical, text, multimedia, time-series, biological, network, and uncertain data). Finally, the book focuses on the appropriateness of a particular clustering method through evaluation techniques available from different variations of cluster analysis (visual, supervised, ensemble, and validation-based solutions).

Ahmed, Nesreen K., Amir F. Atiya, Neamat El Gayar, and Hisham El-Shishiny. 2010. "An Empirical Comparison of Machine Learning Models for Time Series Forecasting." *Econometric Reviews* 29 (5–6): 594–621. https://doi.org/10.1080/07474938.2010.481556.

The authors conduct a comparative analysis of the forecasting performance of several ML methods (multilayer perceptron, Bayesian neural networks, radial basis functions, generalized regression neural networks, K-nearest neighbor regression, classification and regression trees, SVR, and Gaussian process) for time-series data. Using a monthly time-series data sample, the results show that multilayer perceptron and the Gaussian process regression outperform the other ML methods considered, indicating that the rarely used Gaussian process method may offer performance improvement in forecasting problems.

Ahn, Jae Joon, Kyong Joo Oh, Tae Yoon Kim, and Dong Ha Kim. 2011. "Usefulness of Support Vector Machine to Develop an Early Warning System for Financial Crisis." *Expert Systems with Applications* 38 (4): 2966–73. https://doi.org/10.1016/j.eswa.2010.08.085.

Existing studies on early warning systems for financial crises are based on a belief system that considers financial crises to be self-fulfilling as a result of investor herding behavior. In this article, the authors take the alternative view that banking crises result from deteriorating long-term economic fundamentals. With this new hypothesis, the authors find that SVM is an effective technique for this classification problem.

Alberg, John, and Zachary C. Lipton. 2017. "Improving Factor-Based Quantitative Investing by Forecasting Company Fundamentals," version 2. arXiv.org/abs/1711.04837v2.

Fundamental financial data of publicly traded companies, such as operating income, revenue, assets, dividends, and debt, provide a picture of those companies' financial performance. If the future fundamentals can be forecasted, then an investment strategy can build portfolios based on the predicted fundamentals that can outperform a standard factor approach. Using data on stocks for publicly traded US companies, the authors develop and forecast features from the fundamentals and evaluate the out-of-sample forecasting performance using two classes of DNNs (multilayer perceptrons and recurrent neural networks). This lookahead factor model with DNNs significantly outperforms the naive prediction (i.e., fundamentals remain unchanged). In addition, a simulated hypothetical stock portfolio using an industry-grade stock portfolio simulator shows a performance improvement over traditional factor models in terms of compounded annual returns.

Allen, Franklin, and Risto Karjalainen. 1999. "Using Genetic Algorithms to Find Technical Trading Rules." *Journal of Financial Economics* 51 (2): 245–71. https://doi.org/:10.1016/S0304-405X(98)00052-X.

In this article, the authors examine the S&P 500 composite index from 1928 to 1995 to generate trading rules using genetic algorithms. Similar to what past findings have revealed, trading rules created by genetic algorithms do not make money after controlling for transaction costs. Genetic algorithm-based trading rules can correctly identify periods of high return and low volatility and periods with opposite conditions.

Alpaydin, Ethem. 2010. *Introduction to Machine Learning*, 2nd ed. Cambridge, MA: MIT Press.

This introductory textbook on ML covers relevant algorithms and methods from computer science, neural computation, and statistics. The topics include, but are not limited to, supervised learning, Bayesian decision theory and Bayesian estimation, parametric and nonparametric methods, multivariate methods, dimensionality reduction, decision trees, linear discrimination, kernel machines, hidden Markov models, graphical models, combining multiple learners, reinforcement learning (RL), and the design and analysis of ML experiments.

Arrieta-ibarra, Imanol, and Ignacio N. Lobato. 2015. "Testing for Predictability in Financial Returns Using Statistical Learning Procedures." *Journal of Time Series Analysis* 36 (5): 672–86. https://doi.org/10.1111/jtsa.12120.

The authors examine and compare the out-of-sample forecasting performance of three ML techniques (regression trees, neural networks, and SVMs) with that of a traditional GARCH(1,1) model in predicting daily stock market returns. They conclude that in terms of predictive accuracy, the three ML techniques do not outperform naive historical sample average returns when only past values of the series are considered. Adding other variables (interest rates, commodity prices, or exchange rates) to the model may lead to model overfitting and insignificant results. However, SVMs and neural networks offer potential improvements over a GARCH(1,1) model only for forecasting squared returns.

Atsalakis, George S., and Kimon P. Valavanis. 2009. "Surveying Stock Market Forecasting Techniques – Part II: Soft Computing Methods." *Expert Systems with Applications* 36 (3): 5932–41. http://doi.org/10.1016/j.eswa.2008.07.006.

The authors provide a survey of the literature on stock return forecasting in different markets, revealing that recently, soft computing techniques have increasingly been used for predicting stock market behavior. Neural networks, fuzzy logic, and genetic algorithm are some examples of soft computing techniques. In the prior literature on stock return forecasting, soft computing techniques generally outperform traditional models in terms of forecast accuracy.

Auria, Laura, and Rouslan A. Moro. 2008. "Support Vector Machines (SVM) as a Technique for Solvency Analysis." DIW Berlin Discussion Paper No. 811 (August). https://ssrn.com/abstract=1424949.

The authors propose the use of SVMs in predicting company solvency. Using data on German companies, the SVM technique outperforms alternative approaches, such as logistic regression and discriminant analysis, in out-of-sample accuracy.

Avramov, Doron, Si Cheng, and Lior Metzker. 2019. "Machine Learning versus Economic Restrictions: Evidence from Stock Return Predictability." https://ssrn.com/abstract=3450322.

The researchers argue that ML methods, such as deep learning, often do not clear economic restrictions the way that value-weighting returns, excluding microcaps or distressed firms, do. When economic restrictions are imposed, value-weighted portfolio returns decline relative to equal-weighted portfolio returns. Upon further economic restrictions, the value-weighted portfolio returns attenuate further once microcaps, non-rated firms, and distressed firms are excluded. In the presence of transaction costs, performance may further deteriorate. Nevertheless, ML methods are useful, especially in long positions and because of their low downside risk.

Azimi, Mehran, and Anup Agrawal. 2019. "Is Positive Sentiment in Corporate Annual Reports Informative? Evidence from Deep Learning." https://ssrn.com/abstract=3258821.

The authors use deep learning for text classification of qualitative information found in corporate annual reports. The research findings indicate that, unlike findings in prior literature, both positive and negative sentiments are important in predicting abnormal returns and abnormal trading volume around 10-K filing dates. For instance, positive (negative) sentiment is associated with higher (lower) abnormal returns and with lower (higher) abnormal trading volume around 10-K filing dates.

Aziz, Saqib, and Michael Dowling. 2019. "Machine Learning and AI for Risk Management." In *Disrupting Finance: FinTech and Strategy in the 21st Century*, edited by Theo Lynn, John G. Mooney, Pierangelo Rosati, and Mark Cummins, 33–50. Cham, Switzerland: Palgrave Pivot. https://doi.org/10.1007/978-3-030-02330-0_3.

The authors provide an overview of the application of ML and AI techniques in the risk management domain. They review the relevant literature and discuss the particular techniques used in the areas of credit risk, market risk, operational risk, and compliance.

Ballings, Michel, Dirk Van den Poel, Nathalie Hespeels, and Ruben Gryp. 2015. "Evaluating Multiple Classifiers for Stock Price Direction Prediction." *Expert Systems with Applications* 42 (20): 7046–56. https://doi.org/10.1016/j.eswa.2015.05.013.

In this study, the authors compare ensemble ML methods (Random Forest, AdaBoost, Kernel Factory) with single classifiers (Neural Networks, Logistic Regression, Support Vector Machines, K-Nearest Neighbor) with respect to their ability to predict the direction of stock price movements. Based on AUC (areas under the receiver operating characteristic curve) as a performance measure, the algorithms are ranked as follows: Random Forests, Support Vector Machines, Kernel Factory, AdaBoost, Neural Networks, K-Nearest Neighbor, and Logistic Regression. The study concludes that ensemble models should not be neglected in predicting stock price direction.

Bao, Yang, and Anindya Datta. 2014. "Simultaneously Discovering and Quantifying Risk Types from Textual Risk Disclosures." *Management Science* 60 (6): 1371–91. https://doi.org/10.1287/mnsc.2014.1930.

The authors use a latent Dirichlet allocation topic model to simultaneously identify and measure the risk types from risk disclosure information in 10-K forms. Empirical results indicate that the presented textual analysis method outperforms all competing methods. Further, the proposed technique identifies that only one-third of risk types are informative. Among the risk types that are found to be informative, only systematic and liquidity-related risks will increase investors' risk perceptions, whereas nonsystematic risk types will actually decrease them.

Becker, Sebastian, Patrick Cheridito, and Arnulf Jentzen. 2019a. "Deep Optimal Stopping." *Journal of Machine Learning Research* 20: 1–25.

In this article, the authors develop an optimal stopping strategy using deep learning. They construct lower and upper bounds, point estimates, and confidence intervals for the price. The authors then test the approach in three different examples: the pricing of a Bermudan max-call option, the pricing of a callable multi-barrier reverse convertible, and the problem of optimally stopping a fractional Brownian motion. The results show that in all three exercises, the proposed method produces highly accurate results with short computing times.

Becker, Sebastian, Patrick Cheridito, and Arnulf Jentzen. 2019b. "Pricing and Hedging American-Style Options with Deep Learning." https://arxiv.org/abs/1912.11060.

In this article, the authors consider American-style options and develop a DNN for optimal exercise behavior, pricing, and hedging. In the first stage, the neural network method is used to find the optimal stopping rule and derive a lower bound estimate of the price. In the next stage, it estimates an upper bound and confidence intervals for the price. Finally, the deep learning method constructs a dynamic hedging strategy. Exercises based on Bermudan max-call options show that the proposed method can achieve accurate price predictions and provide dynamic hedging strategies.

Beketov, Mikhail, Kevin Lehmann, and Manuel Wittke. 2018. "Robo Advisors: Quantitative Methods Inside the Robots." *Journal of Asset Management* 19: 363–70. http://doi.org/10.1057/s41260-018-0092-9.

The authors explore the methods of robo-advisors around the world and find modern portfolio theory to be the predominant method used in robo-advisory systems. Further, the volume of assets managed by robo-advisors is likely to be higher when more sophisticated systems are used.

Bellovary, Jodi L., Don E. Giacomino, and Michael D. Akers. 2007. "A Review of Bankruptcy Prediction Studies: 1930 to Present." *Journal of Financial Education* 33: 1–42.

For this study, the authors review bankruptcy prediction literature published since the 1930s. Bankruptcy prediction studies in earlier years primarily used simple ratio analysis, whereas discriminant analysis became more prevalent in the 1960s and 1970s. In the 1980s and 1990s, logit and neural networks methods gained more popularity in bankruptcy analysis. Comparisons of different methods reveal that multivariate discriminant analysis and neural networks deliver better bankruptcy prediction models. In addition, the authors note that a model's accuracy may not always increase with the number of factors used in the model.

Bertsimas, Dimitris, and Andrew W. Lo. 1998. "Optimal Control of Execution Costs." *Journal of Financial Markets* 1 (1): 1–50. https://doi.org/10.1016/S1386-4181(97)00012-8.

The performance of investments is affected by the presence of trading or execution costs, which include commissions, bid–ask spreads, and opportunity costs. In this article, the authors present a dynamic trading strategy that seeks to minimize expected trading costs. The cost-minimizing strategy is a function of time and several state variables, so it can optimally adapt to changing market conditions and price movements. Compared with a naive trading strategy, the best-execution strategy reduces execution costs by 25% to 40%.

Berutich, José Manuel, Francisco López, Francisco Luna, and David Quintana. 2016. "Robust Technical Trading Strategies Using GP for Algorithmic Portfolio Selection." *Expert Systems with Applications* 46 (15): 307–15. https://doi.org/10.1016/j.eswa.2015.10.040.

The authors of this study examine a genetic algorithm approach for generating profitable trading rules in the Spanish market. The article's main contribution is the introduction of a new random sampling method that improves the out-of-sample results of the genetic algorithm compared with traditional approaches. This method can also be generalized to cope with different types of markets. Empirical tests of the strategies generated using this approach confirm the superiority of the approach over a range of traditional alternatives.

Bew, David, Campbell R. Harvey, Anthony Ledford, Sam Radnor, and Andrew Sinclair. 2019. "Modeling Analysts' Recommendations via Bayesian Machine Learning." *Journal of Financial Data Science* 1 (1): 75–98.

Individual analysts focus on only a small number of thousands of companies in making recommendations on stock performance. In this study, the authors propose a novel approach for combining individual analyst recommendations using an independent Bayesian classifier combination (IBCC) model that dynamically adjusts based on the length and quality of an analyst's track record. The forecasts are obtained from the probabilistic IBCC model using data from the pan-European region from 2004 to 2013. The results indicate that the best outcome is achieved when the analyst/broker recommendation is consistent with forecasts from the IBCC model.

Bholat, David M., Stephen Hansen, Pedro Santos, and Cheryl Schonhardt-Bailey. 2015. "Text Mining for Central Banks." http://dx.doi.org/10.2139/ssrn.2624811.

Text mining can be used to extract meaning from texts. This handbook illustrates the value of text mining methods to central banks. The first part of the handbook reviews the text mining literature, examining how it could be applied to central bank policymaking. The second part explains the implementation of popular text mining techniques, such as Boolean and dictionary text mining, latent semantic analysis, latent Dirichlet allocation, and descending hierarchical classification.

Bianchi, Daniele, Matthias Büchner, and Andrea Tamoni. 2019. "Bond Risk Premia with Machine Learning." https://doi.org/10.2139/ssrn.3400941.

The authors compare the performance of ML methods in predicting bond returns. Compared with classical approaches, such as dense and sparse linear regression frameworks, DNNs perform significantly better in forecasting excess bond returns. Empirical exercises using both one-year-ahead and one-month-ahead forecasts show that neural networks outperform other classical approaches largely because of their ability to capture nonlinearities in the data.

Black, Fischer, and Robert Litterman. 1992. "Global Portfolio Optimization." *Financial Analysts Journal* 48 (5): 28–43. https://doi.org/10.2469/faj.v48.n5.28.

In this article, the authors discuss the limitations of modern portfolio management theory in global portfolio management. The main limitation of classic portfolio management theory is the difficulty of its implementation and its unexpected poor behavior when used for global portfolios. The authors suggest combining Markowitz's mean–variance portfolio optimization model with the CAPM of Sharpe and Lintner to improve the portfolio allocation behavior.

Board of Governors of the Federal Reserve System. 2011. "Supervisory Guidance on Model Risk Management." Office of the Comptroller of the

Currency (April 4). https://www.occ.treas.gov/news-issuances/bulletins/2011/bulletin-2011-12a.pdf.

Financial institutions have been using models in many aspects of banking, but models also carry risks and costs. This paper presents an overview of model risk management, robust model development, model validation, and good practices in model development, implementation, and application.

Booth, Ash, Enrico Gerding, and Frank McGroarty. 2014. "Automated Trading with Performance Weighted Random Forests and Seasonality." *Expert Systems with Applications* 41 (8): 3651–61. https://doi.org/10.1016/j.eswa.2013.12.009.

The authors of this study present an automated trading system based on performance-weighted ensembles of random forests. The proposed method uses seasonal trends to improve the predictability of stock returns. Using data on the German stock index DAX, the proposed new technique shows promising results for out-of-sample forecasts. Specifically, it achieves better prediction accuracy and higher profitability than other ensemble methods.

Booth, Ash, Enrico Gerding, and Frank McGroarty. 2015. "Performance-Weighted Ensembles of Random Forests for Predicting Price Impact." *Quantitative Finance* 15 (11): 1823–35. https://doi.org/10.1080/14697688.2014.983539.

In this study, the researchers present a forecasting model based on an ensemble of random forests. The empirical results show that the proposed model outperforms other popular competing models—linear regression, neural networks, and SVR—in out-of-sample forecasts. The ensemble of random forests improves forecast accuracy by at least 15% compared with the competing models.

Borghi, Riccardo, and Giuliano De Rossi. Forthcoming. "The Artificial Intelligence Approach to Picking Stocks." In *Machine Learning and Asset Management*. Cham, Switzerland: Springer.

The chapter's authors explore ML techniques to select from a large set of firm characteristics to predict one-month-ahead stock returns using data for US and European stocks. They use a proprietary alpha model, a global stock selection model from Macquarie, as a benchmark for comparing the results from traditional ML techniques (ordinary least squares, generalized linear model, LASSO, ridge, elastic net, neural networks, boosted trees and random forest, and regression trees). The results indicate that an ensemble of ML methods could outperform even a proprietary model with a successful track record, such as Macquarie's Alpha Quant model, in terms of generating attractive risk–return ratios. However, ML tend to be less exposed to price momentum than alpha models are.

Branke, Juergen, Benedikt Scheckenbach, Michael Stein, Kalyanmoy Deb, and Hartmut Schmeck. 2009. "Portfolio Optimization with an Envelope-Based Multi-Objective Evolutionary Algorithm." *European Journal of Operational Research* 199 (3): 684–93. https://doi.org/10.1016/j.ejor.2008.01.054.

The mean–variance-based portfolio optimization problem with linear constraints can be solved efficiently using parametric quadratic programming. Many real-world constraints tend to be more complex and discrete, however, such as when the number of stocks in a portfolio is limited. In this study, the authors combine parametric quadratic programming with a multi-objective evolutionary algorithm to find the best solution to the nonconvex portfolio selection. As the results demonstrate, the proposed multi-objective evolutionary algorithm model significantly outperforms other existing evolutionary algorithms.

Breiman, Leo. 2001. "Random Forests." *Machine Learning* 45 (1): 5–32. https://doi.org/10.1023/A:1010933404324.

In this seminal work, the author introduces random forests, which are collections of tree predictors used in a classification problem. As the number of trees increase and given the law of large numbers, random forests do not suffer from overfitting problems and are an effective forecasting tool used in ML.

Brenner, Lukas, and Tobias Meyll. 2019. "Robo-Advisors: A Substitute for Human Financial Advice?" https://ssrn.com/abstract=3414200.

With recent technological advances in the financial services industry, the use of automated financial advisors (i.e., robo-advisors) has been increasing. The authors investigate the determinants of investor decisions to opt for robo-advisory services. Using representative investor survey data, the authors show that a significant substitution is taking place because investors are worried about potential conflicts of interest with human financial advisors.

Briere, Marie, Charles-Albert Lehalle, Tamara Nefedova, and Amine Raboun. 2019. "Modelling Transaction Costs When Trades May Be Crowded: A Bayesian Network Using Partially Observable Orders Imbalance." https://ssrn.com/abstract=3420665.

The authors use a Bayesian network model to forecast transaction costs measured as implementation shortfall. The Bayesian network approach can account for missing data by using the most probable values instead. This feature is particularly useful for integrating important latent variables, such as the net order flow imbalance of investors to improve the transaction cost forecasts. The findings suggest that implementation shortfall forecasts are more accurate when investors' order size is larger or when stock volatility is lower.

Bryzgalova, Svetlana, Markus Pelger, and Jason Zhu. 2019. "Forest Through the Trees: Building Cross-Sections of Stock Returns." https://ssrn.com/abstract=3493458.

The authors describe a new method of building basis assets that capture the underlying information in the cross-sections of asset returns. The novel approach allows us to capture the complex information of cross-sectional stock characteristics. The proposed method applies asset-pricing trees to build portfolios that capture all relevant information, allow for nonlinearities and interactions, act as building blocks for a stochastic discount factor, and provide test assets for asset pricing. The empirical results using monthly equity returns for all CRSP securities show that, unlike the proposed approach, conventional cross-sectional sorting methods fail to fully capture the relevant information on stock characteristics.

Buchanan, Bonnie G. 2019. "Artificial Intelligence in Finance." http://doi.org/10.5281/zenodo.2612537.

In this literature review, the author overviews AI, ML, and deep learning (DL) and their applications in the financial services sector. She first discusses how rapidly growing AI is changing the financial services industry by using ML algorithms to analyze millions of data points to detect fraudulent activity, by using "robo-advising" that avoids human interaction and conflict of interest, and by using algorithmic trading to make fast trading decisions. The author then discusses the differences between ML and econometrics and the applications of each. Specifically, ML and DL methods focus on predictive accuracy, whereas econometric methods are mainly concerned with inferential questions. ML and DL techniques have become powerful tools for out-of-sample forecasts and for identifying the most useful predictors. Further, the author briefly reviews quantum computing and how it can process data at speeds impossible for traditional computers. Finally, as AI and ML are increasingly applied in the financial services industry, regulators are having difficulty keeping pace with the new technology.

Celik, Arzum Erken, and Yalcin Karatepe. 2007. "Evaluating and Forecasting Banking Crises Through Neural Network Models: An Application for Turkish Banking Sector." *Expert Systems with Applications* 33 (4): 809–15. https://doi.org/10.1016/j.eswa.2006.07.005.

The authors of this study forecast the ratios of nonperforming loans to total loans, capital to assets, profits to assets, and equity to assets for the Turkish banking sector. The results indicate that ANNs that use the Taguchi approach to determine the optimal values of ANN parameters are an effective tool in forecasting banking crises.

Chapados, Nicolas, and Yoshua Bengio. 2001. "Cost Functions and Model Combination for VaR-Based Asset Allocation Using Neural Networks." *IEEE Transactions on Neural Networks* 12 (4): 890–906. https://doi.org/10.1109/72.935098.

The authors consider value at risk (VaR), typically used in quantifying the risk associated with a portfolio, and extend it to the mean–VaR framework, similar in spirit to Markowitz's famous mean–variance model. Mean–VaR seeks to find the best portfolio allocation for a given VaR level. The authors build neural networks to optimize the portfolio of assets given the VaR constraint and transaction costs and show that the portfolio's performance is comparable to that of a forecasting model based on the classical mean–variance portfolio management but better than that of the benchmark market index. However, the proposed method relies on fewer model assumptions and takes transaction costs into account. Finally, both the proposed and the classical forecasting models can significantly outperform the benchmark market index when a forecast combination technique is applied.

Chen, Luyang, Markus Pelger, and Jason Zhu. 2020. "Deep Learning in Asset Pricing." https://ssrn.com/abstract=3350138.

The article's authors use DNNs and a no-arbitrage constraint to estimate individual stock returns. Specifically, they combine three different neural networks (feedforward network, long–short-term-memory network, generative adversarial network) with a no-arbitrage condition to estimate the stochastic discount factor that explains stock returns. The stochastic discount factor portfolio uses time-varying weights for traded assets, which are functions of firm-specific and macroeconomic variables. The proposed stochastic discount factor asset pricing model outperforms other benchmark models out of sample.

Chen, Shiyi, Wolfgang K. Hardle, and Kiho Jeong. 2009. "Forecasting Volatility with Support Vector Machine-Based GARCH Model." *Journal of Forecasting* 29 (4): 406–33.

The study authors compare the volatility forecasts generated from the traditional volatility forecasting methods (moving average, GARCH, exponential generalized autoregressive conditional heteroskedasticity [EGARCH], ANN-GARCH) with the forecasts obtained using an SVM or ANN. Using a recursive forecasting framework, one-step-ahead forecasts of the volatilities of the British exchange rate and NYSE index are evaluated based on the Diebold–Mariano forecast evaluation method. Of all the models considered, SVM-GARCH models perform well in many cases, whereas a standard GARCH model performs well when the sample size is large and normally distributed. On the other hand, an EGARCH model better predicts the one-step ahead volatility when the data are highly skewed.

Chen, Wun-Hua, Jen-Ying Shih, and Soushan Wu. 2006. "Comparison of Support-Vector Machines and Back Propagation Neural Networks in Forecasting the Six Major Asian Stock Markets." *International Journal of Electronic Finance* 1 (1): 49–67. https://doi.org/10.1504/IJEF.2006.008837.

Most of the existing research in the application of data mining techniques to financial time series forecasting focuses on the US or European markets. The authors of this study examine the performance of SVM and back propagation neural networks in forecasting six Asian stock markets. Compared with naive autoregressive (1) time-series models, both proposed models perform well.

Cheng, Ching-Hsue, Tai-Liang Chen, and Liang-Ying Wei. 2010. "A Hybrid Model Based on Rough Sets Theory and Genetic Algorithms for Stock Price Forecasting." *Information Sciences* 180 (9): 1610–29. https://doi.org/10.1016/j.ins.2010.01.014.

Professional fund managers do not easily understand time-series forecasting methods and AI techniques used in forecasting stock returns. Therefore, they often rely on subjective judgments in predicting stock prices based on some technical indicators. The authors develop a hybrid forecasting framework that uses the tools of rough set theory and genetic algorithms. Empirical results show that the proposed hybrid techniques outperform the rough set theory and genetic algorithms in terms of forecast accuracy and profits.

Chinco, Alexander M., Adam D. Clark-Joseph, and Mao Ye. 2019. "Sparse Signals in the Cross-Section of Returns." *Journal of Finance* 74 (1): 449–92. https://doi.org/10.1111/jofi.12733.

Using LASSO, a penalized regression technique, the authors study the out-of-sample fit of one-minute-ahead return forecasts. Evidence suggests that this improved performance mainly results from the identification of predictors that are unexpected, short lived, and sparse. Further, the LASSO method is found to increase the forecast-implied Sharpe ratio.

Choudhry, Taufiq, Frank McGroarty, Ke Peng, and Shiyun Wang. 2012. "High-Frequency Exchange-Rate Prediction with an Artificial Neural Network." *Intelligent Systems in Accounting, Finance & Management* 19 (3): 170–78. https://doi.org/10.1002/isaf.1329.

The authors study the effectiveness of ANN for forecasting high-frequency exchange rates, ranging from one minute to a few minutes. They find that bid and ask prices are significant variables for exchange rate forecasting. The study concludes that high-frequency trading strategies using ANNs can generate positive profit beyond transaction costs.

Cong, Lin, Tengyuan Liang, and Xiao Zhang. 2019. "Textual Factors: A Scalable, Interpretable, and Data-Driven Approach to Analyzing Unstructured Information." https://ssrn.com/abstract=3307057.

Increased access to unstructured data in the form of texts can be used to complement information obtained from the traditional structured data. Extracting insight from textual data is more complex, however, because of the data's intricate language structure and high dimensionality, and because of the lack of data-driven approaches to analyzing textual data. The authors develop an alternative method of analyzing textual data that is more effective than the existing methods. They use neural network models for NLP to generate textual factors and show the procedure's application in analyzing financial and macroeconomic data.

Coqueret, Guillaume, and Tony Guida. 2018. "Stock Returns and the Cross-Section of Characteristics: A Tree-Based Approach." https://ssrn.com/abstract=3169773.

The authors use regression trees that iteratively split the sample into clusters so they can investigate the effects of 30 classical firm characteristics on future returns. Unlike linear regression models, tree-based regression models take into account the conditional impact of firm attributes given the value of other attributes. The findings indicate that both technical indicators (e.g., the Relative Strength Index) and past performance indicators are important in stock pricing. The authors estimate that a portfolio built using a short-term Relative Strength Index characteristic leads to an annual gain of 2.4% relative to a naive, equally weighted portfolio.

Cortes, Corinna, and Vladimir Vapnik. 1995. "Support-Vector Networks." *Machine Learning* 20 (3): 273–97. https://doi.org/10.1007/BF00994018.

The support-vector network is an ML algorithm used in classification problems with two groups. The authors generalize the support-vector networks for separable training data and extend the algorithm to nonseparable training data.

D'Acunto, Francesco, Nagpurnanand Prabhala, and Alberto Rossi. 2017. "The Promises and Pitfalls of Robo-Advising." https://ssrn.com/abstract=3122577.

The authors investigate the use of robo-advising in portfolio management. Investors who use robo-advising tend to have more assets, trade more often, and have better risk-adjusted performance. The results show that among investors who adopt robo-advising, diversification and stock volatility decrease when the number of stocks held is less than five. The same is not true, however, when the number of stocks initially held is more than 10. Thus, the study illustrates the possible heterogeneous impacts of robo-advising on investors' portfolio performance.

Das, Sanjiv Ranjan. 2014. "Text and Context: Language Analytics in Finance." *Foundations and Trends in Finance* 8 (3): 145–261. https://doi.org/10.1561/0500000045.

In this monograph, the author provides a comprehensive survey of techniques and applications of text analytics in the field of finance. Specifically, he discusses text extraction steps using the statistical package R, how to analyze the extracted text, the classification of texts and words, and the application of text data in empirical studies.

DeMiguel, Victor, Lorenzo Garlappi, and Raman Uppal. 2009. "Optimal versus Naive Diversification: How Inefficient Is the 1/*N* Portfolio Strategy?" *Review of Financial Studies* 22 (5): 1915–53. https://doi.org/10.1093/rfs/hhm075.

The authors conduct an empirical exercise to evaluate the out-of-sample performance of optimal asset allocation models. In terms of Sharpe ratio, certainty equivalent return, and turnover, none of these models fared better than the naive 1/*N* portfolio. The authors attribute this finding to model estimation error that more than offsets the gains from optimal portfolio diversification.

Dhar, Vasant, and Roger Stein. 2017. "FinTech Platforms and Strategy." MIT Sloan Research Paper No. 5183-16. https://ssrn.com/abstract=2892098.

Briefly, fintech is described as financial sector innovations that have revolutionized most aspects of financial services. The article's authors discuss the current status of fintech in the internet era, future directions of change, and possible strategies to pursue. The fintech market has yet to achieve its highest potential, because developing countries continue to enter the digital era and new platforms for financial services are still developing.

Dixon, Matthew, Diego Klabjan, and Jin Hoon Bang. 2017. "Classification-Based Financial Markets Prediction Using Deep Neural Networks." *Algorithmic Finance* 6 (3–4): 67–77.

DNNs have been successfully applied to speech transcription and image detection. In this study, the authors describe the application of DNNs to the classification of direction of movement in financial data.

Dixon, Matthew, and Nicholas G. Polson. 2019. "Deep Fundamental Factor Models." https://arxiv.org/abs/1903.07677.

The authors extend fundamental factor models using neural networks to allow for nonlinearity, interaction effects, and nonparametric shocks. The proposed technique can be used under heteroskedastic errors, provides interpretability, and ranks the importance of factors (e.g., current enterprise value, price-to-book ratio, price-to-sales ratio, price-to-earnings ratio, log market cap) and interaction effects. The neural network factor model predicts S&P 500 stock returns with smaller out-of-sample mean-squared errors than generalized linear regressions do. In addition, neural network factor models are found to produce information ratios that are three times higher than those seen with linear models.

Donaldson, R. Glen, and Mark Kamstra. 1997. "An Artificial Neural Network-GARCH Model for International Stock Return Volatility." *Journal of Empirical Finance* 4 (1): 17–46. https://doi.org/10.1016/S0927-5398(96)00011-4.

The authors examine the performance of stock return volatility forecasting models using daily returns data from London, New York, Tokyo, and Toronto. An ANN-GARCH model is found to generally outperform its traditional competing models—GARCH, EGARCH, and Sign-GARCH models—in both in-sample and out-of-sample periods.

Dunis, Christian L., Jason Laws, and Georgios Sermpinis. 2010. "Modelling and Trading the EUR/USD Exchange Rate at the ECB Fixing." *European Journal of Finance* 16 (6): 541–60. https://doi.org/10.1080/13518470903037771.

The authors explore the application of neural networks to the exchange rate forecasting problem. Unlike previous studies on neural networks that select the network's inputs on an ad hoc basis, the neural network techniques in this study use autoregressive terms as inputs. The performance of several such neural network techniques (including a higher-order neural network, a Psi Sigma network, and a neural network with multilayer perceptron) on the daily EUR/USD exchange rate are compared with the performance of traditional methods. In simple simulated exercises, the multilayer perceptron technique significantly outperforms the other models considered. For sophisticated trading strategies, the higher-order neural network technique achieves higher annualized returns than other neural network techniques.

Eiben, Agoston E., and Jim E. Smith. 2015. *Introduction to Evolutionary Computing*, 2nd ed. New York: Springer. https://doi.org/10.1007/978-3-662-44874-8.

The authors of this textbook provide a comprehensive introduction to evolutionary algorithms, from history to major design decisions to parameter tuning and control. Advanced topics include multi-objective optimization, the optimization of dynamic and noisy functions, constraint handling, and hybridization with other techniques.

Elliott, Graham, and Allan Timmermann. 2008. "Economic Forecasting." *Journal of Economic Literature* 46 (1): 3–56. https://doi.org/10.1257/jel.46.1.3.

This study's authors present economic forecasting problems in a unified framework, including forecasters' loss functions and types of economic forecasting methods. The authors then explore the various forecasting methodologies available to researchers, such as optimal point forecasts, a classical approach to forecasting, a Bayesian approach to forecasting, density forecasts, and forecast combination techniques.

Fan, Alan, and Marimuthu Palaniswami. 2001. "Stock Selection Using Support Vector Machines." In *International Joint Conference on Neural Networks. Proceedings (Cat. No. 01CH37222)*, vol. 3, 1793–98. Washington, DC: IEEE.

The authors choose stocks trading on the Australian Securities Exchange using SVM. Compared with the 71% return for the benchmark portfolio, an equally weighted portfolio of stocks selected by SVM produced a 208% return over a five-year period.

Farmer, J. Doyne, Austin Gerig, Fabrizio Lillo, and Szabolcs Mike. 2006. "Market Efficiency and the Long-Memory of Supply and Demand: Is Price Impact Variable and Permanent or Fixed and Temporary?" *Quantitative Finance* 6 (2): 107–12. https://doi.org/10.1080/14697680600668048.

The long-memory of demand and supply means that future buying and selling behavior, and therefore price movements, should be predictable. In reality, however, price movements are essentially uncorrelated. The authors aim to explain market efficiency given these two apparently contradictory facts. They revisit earlier studies on the topic to demonstrate that market efficiency is maintained by liquidity imbalances rather than mean-reverting price changes. To show this dynamic, they introduce transaction time into the model and demonstrate that liquidity covaries in time with the long-memory of supply and demand.

Feng, Guanhao, Stefano Giglio, and Dacheng Xiu. 2017. "Taming the Factor Zoo: A Test of New Factors." Fama-Miller Working Paper; Chicago Booth Research Paper No. 17-04. https://ssrn.com/abstract=2934020.

The authors present a variant of the LASSO method to identify the most relevant factors among many potential candidates to explain asset returns. The results indicate that only a few recently introduced factors, including profitability, have significant incremental explanatory power.

Feng, Guanhao, Nick Polson, and Jianeng Xu. 2020. "Deep Learning in Characteristics-Sorted Factor Models." https://ssrn.com/abstract=3243683.

Unlike the researchers of previous literature, who related firm characteristics (inputs) to security returns (outputs), the authors of this paper introduce an intermediate channel involving risk factors (intermediate features). With the goal of reducing pricing errors, this bottom-up approach trains a neural network that generates risk factors using firm characteristics to explain security returns. The authors provide an alternative dimension reduction framework on security sorting and factor generation.

Fernandes, Marcelo, Marcelo C. Medeiros, and Marcel Scharth. 2014. "Modeling and Predicting the CBOE Market Volatility Index." *Journal of Banking & Finance* 40: 1–10. https://doi.org/10.1016/j.jbankfin.2013.11.004.

The Chicago Board Options Exchange (CBOE) reports the volatility index (VIX) based on the 30-calendar day S&P 500 index option.

This implied volatility, a key indicator of overall market condition, is used in many trading strategies. The authors study the time series properties of the VIX series, showing that the VIX is negatively correlated with S&P 500 returns but has a positive relationship with S&P 500 volume. Further, these two series do not appear to have a nonlinear relationship.

Financial Stability Board. 2017. "Artificial Intelligence and Machine Learning in Financial Services." http://www.fsb.org/2017/11/artificial-intelligence-and-machine-learning-in-financial-service.

This report by the Financial Stability Board examines the implications arising from the application of AI and ML methods in financial services. It presents some background on the recent rise in the use of AI and ML in various finance applications and services, discusses possible effects on the financial system, and assesses risks to its stability. The authors conclude that in the absence of "audibility" and interpretability, AI and ML techniques may pose macro-level risks and should therefore be monitored by microprudential supervisors.

Fischer, Thomas, and Christopher Krauss. 2018. "Deep Learning with Long Short-Term Memory Networks for Financial Market Predictions." *European Journal of Operational Research* 270 (2): 654–69. https://doi.org/10.1016/j.ejor.2017.11.054.

In this study, the authors use long short-term memory (LSTM) networks in predicting out-of-sample movements for S&P 500 stocks. LSTM is a type of sequence learning method specifically designed to learn long-term dependencies. LSTM clearly outperforms memory-free classification methods, such as deep neural nets and a logistic regression, in terms of predictive accuracy. It also beats random forests, except during the global financial crisis.

Fisher, Ingrid E., Margaret R. Garnsey, and Mark E. Hughes. 2016. "Natural Language Processing in Accounting, Auditing and Finance: A Synthesis of the Literature with a Roadmap for Future Research." *Intelligent Systems in Accounting, Finance & Management* 23 (3): 157–214. https://doi.org/10.1002/isaf.1386.

In this article, the authors synthesize the literature that applies NLP in accounting, auditing, and finance. NLP is used to analyze textual data (e.g., corporate financial performance, management's assessment of firm performance, regulations), detect fraud, make inferences, and predict stock prices. The review of large literature in the three fields reveals that of all the ML techniques applied in NLP, SVMs are the most popular tool, followed by Naive Bayes, hierarchical clustering, statistical methods, and term-frequency-inverse document frequency weighting.

Fletcher, Tristan, and John Shawe-Taylor. 2013. "Multiple Kernel Learning with Fisher Kernels for High Frequency Currency Prediction." *Computational Economics* 42: 217–40. https://doi.org/10.1007/s10614-012-9317-z.

The authors construct kernels based on EUR/USD exchange rate data from limited order book volumes, technical analysis, and market microstructure models. With these multiple kernels, SVMs are used to predict the direction of price movements. SVMs based on multiple kernels significantly outperform individual SVMs and achieve 55% forecast accuracy, on average.

Freyberger, Joachim, Andreas Neuhierl, and Michael Weber. 2018. "Dissecting Characteristics Nonparametrically." University of Chicago, Becker Friedman Institute for Economics Working Paper No. 2018-50. https://ssrn.com/abstract=3223630.

The authors propose a nonparametric method for choosing firm characteristics that have incremental predictive power for the cross-section of stock returns. Using an adaptive LASSO nonparametric method for model selection and stock return forecast, they find that of 62 firm characteristics, only 9–16 have incremental predictive power. Compared with linear model selection methods, LASSO performs relatively well in both model selection and expected return predictors.

Geva, Tomer, and Jacob Zahavi. 2014. "Empirical Evaluation of an Automated Intraday Stock Recommendation System Incorporating Both Market Data and Textual News." *Decision Support Systems* 57: 212–23. https://doi.org/10.1016/j.dss.2013.09.013.

The authors examine the effectiveness of incorporating textual news data for stock return forecasting. To this end, various textual data types are added sequentially to numerical market data to study the incremental gain in forecasting performance. Overall, integrating textual data with market data and using neural networks significantly improve forecast accuracy.

Giamouridis, Daniel. 2017. "Systematic Investment Strategies." *Financial Analysts Journal* 73 (4): 10–14. https://doi.org/10.2469/faj.v73.n4.10.

The author offers some thoughts on the latest research on systematic investment from both academic and practical perspectives, also highlighting areas where further research can improve the practice more considerably. The article's topics include data science and ML, factor investing, market timing, and coordinated investing and holding.

Giamouridis, Daniel, and Sandra Paterlini. 2010. "Regular(ized) Hedge Fund Clones." *Journal of Financial Research* 33 (3): 223–47. https://doi.org/10.1111/j.1475-6803.2010.01269.x.

The authors show the attractiveness of using constrained portfolio optimization methods for constructing efficient hedge fund clones. The findings indicate that the proposed hedge fund portfolio is competitive relative to hedge fund clones obtained by commercially available proprietary construction techniques as well as by benchmark hedge fund indices. The replicated hedge fund portfolio exhibits a very high correlation with the benchmark indices.

Gogas, Periklis, Theophilos Papadimitriou, Maria Matthaiou, and Efthymia Chrysanthidou. 2015. "Yield Curve and Recession Forecasting in a Machine Learning Framework." *Computational Economics* 45: 635–45. https://doi.org/10.1007/s10614-014-9432-0.

The authors demonstrate the superior forecasting performance of SVMs in forecasting economic recessions in the United States. Compared with logit and probit models, the SVM technique improves forecast accuracy by 67%–100%.

Gradojevic, Nikola, and Jing Yang. 2006. "Non-Linear, Non-Parametric, Non-Fundamental Exchange Rate Forecasting." *Journal of Forecasting* 25 (4): 227–45. https://doi.org/10.1002/for.986.

The authors examine the exchange rate forecasting performance of ANNs. Compared with naive random walk models and linear time series models, ANNs perform well in forecasting the CAD/USD exchange rate based on the root mean squared error criterion.

Groth, Sven S., and Jan Muntermann. 2011. "An Intraday Market Risk Management Approach Based on Textual Analysis." *Decision Support Systems* 50 (4): 680–91. https://doi.org/10.1016/j.dss.2010.08.019.

The authors study the potential gains from using newly obtained qualitative text data to explain intraday market risk. Using Naive Bayes, K-nearest neighbor, neural network, and SVMs for textual analysis, the authors conclude that these techniques are helpful in discovering intraday market exposure, with the latter model (SVM) being the best in terms of computational efficiency and classification accuracy.

Gu, Shihao, Bryan T. Kelly, and Dacheng Xiu. 2020. "Empirical Asset Pricing via Machine Learning." *Review of Financial Studies* 33 (5): 2223–73.

The authors show that ML techniques (trees and neural nets) may outperform traditional cross-section and time-series models in predicting asset risk premia. The gain in predictive performance comes from the ability of ML methods to allow nonlinear predictive interactions that may be infeasible with traditional statistical methods.

Gu, Shihao, Bryan T. Kelly, and Dacheng Xiu. 2019. "Autoencoder Asset Pricing Models." Yale ICF Working Paper No. 2019-04; Chicago Booth Research Paper No. 19-24. https://ssrn.com/abstract=3335536.

The study's authors propose an autoencoder neural network latent factor modeling for asset pricing. Although other studies incorporate a linearity assumption, the authors' approach allows for nonlinear relationships between factor exposures and asset characteristics. Incorporating the no-arbitrage condition into the ML framework, the new latent factor asset pricing model produces far smaller out-of-sample errors relative to other leading asset pricing modeling techniques, such as Fama–French, principal component analysis, and linear conditioning methods.

Hagenau, Michael, Michael Liebmann, and Dirk Neumann. 2013. "Automated News Reading: Stock Price Prediction Based on Financial News Using Context-Capturing Features." *Decision Support Systems* 55 (3): 685–97. https://doi.org/10.1016/j.dss.2013.02.006.

In this article, the authors describe the application of textual financial information to stock price prediction. Unlike other, similar approaches, the one in this study uses a feature selection that allows market feedback. By selecting the feedback-based relevant features, the approach reduces overfitting problems and significantly improves classification accuracy. As a result, stock return prediction accuracy increased by as much as 76%.

Hamid, Shaikh A., and Zahid Iqbal. 2004. "Using Neural Networks for Forecasting Volatility of S&P 500 Index Futures Prices." *Journal of Business Research* 57 (10): 1116–25. https://doi.org/10.1016/S0148-2963(03)00043-2.

The authors of this study examine the performance of the popular neural networks technique in forecasting the volatility of S&P 500 Index futures prices. The results show that volatility forecasts from neural networks outperform implied volatility forecasts obtained from the Barone–Adesi and Whaley American futures options pricing model.

Han, Shuo, and Rung-Ching Chen. 2007. "Using SVM with Financial Statement Analysis for Prediction of Stocks." *Communications of the IIMA* 7 (4): article 8.

The authors propose applying SVMs to financial statement analysis for stock market prediction. Using financial indices improves forecast accuracy and is more reliable than using technical indices.

Haykin, Simon. 2009. *Neural Networks and Learning Machines*, 3rd ed. New York: Pearson.

In this comprehensive textbook, the author presents an up-to-date treatment of neural networks. The book consists of six main parts that focus on supervised learning, kernel methods based on radial-basis function networks, regularization methods, unsupervised learning, RL, and nonlinear feedback systems.

Heaton, James B., Nick G. Polson, and Jan H. Witte. 2017. "Deep Learning for Finance: Deep Portfolios." *Applied Stochastic Models in Business and Industry* 33 (1): 3–12. https://doi.org/10.1002/asmb.2209.

Traditional prediction and classification methods from financial economics might be impractical or difficult to apply to financial problems, given the large and complex nature of data. The authors describe DL hierarchical models that can improve performance in financial prediction problems and classification.

Hendricks, Dieter, and Diane Wilcox. 2014. "A Reinforcement Learning Extension to the Almgren–Chriss Framework for Optimal Trade Execution." In *2014 IEEE Conference on Computational Intelligence for Financial Engineering & Economics (CIFEr)*, 457–64. London: IEEE.

The authors present an RL technique to optimize the liquidation volume trajectory. The model is based on a standard Almgren–Chriss model, a popular trade execution strategy that assumes risk aversion to trade execution. The proposed technique is able to change the volume of trade using information on market spread and volume dynamics. Empirical tests show promising results. Specifically, on average, the new technique can improve post-trade implementation shortfall by up to 10.3% relative to the base model.

Hong, Taeho, and Ingoo Han. 2002. "Knowledge-Based Data Mining of News Information on the Internet Using Cognitive Maps and Neural Networks." *Expert Systems with Applications* 23 (1): 1–8. https://doi.org/10.1016/S0957-4174(02)00022-2.

The authors of this study create the Knowledge-Based News Miner (KBNMiner), which integrates cognitive maps with neural networks. Unlike the time-series models used in interest rate forecasting, the technique uses prior news on interest rates in predicting interest rates. Relative to neural network and random walk models, KBNMiner leads to improved interest rate predictions.

Hu, Yong, Kang Liu, Xiangzhou Zhang, Lijun Su, E.W.T. Ngai, and Mei Liu. 2015. "Application of Evolutionary Computation for Rule Discovery in Stock Algorithmic Trading: A Literature Review." *Applied Soft Computing* 36: 534–51. https://doi.org/10.1016/j.asoc.2015.07.008.

The authors explore the literature on the application of evolutionary computation in stock algorithmic trading. They observe that most of the trading techniques considered in the surveyed studies do well in the downtrend but poorly in the uptrend, which is likely because of the problems associated with the selection of factors and the transaction costs.

Huang, Chien-Feng. 2012. "A Hybrid Stock Selection Model Using Genetic Algorithms and Support Vector Regression." *Applied Soft Computing* 12 (2): 807–18. https://doi.org/10.1016/j.asoc.2011.10.009.

Stock selection problems are particularly challenging in the area of investment research. This author examines a hybrid approach for stock selection using SVR and genetic algorithms. In the first stage, SVR chooses the top-ranked stocks. In the second stage, genetic algorithms are used to optimize the portfolio parameters and feature selection. The results indicate that this hybrid approach significantly outperforms the benchmark model.

Huang, Wei, Yoshiteru Nakamori, and Shou-Yang Wang. 2005. "Forecasting Stock Market Movement Direction with Support Vector Machine." *Computers & Operations Research* 32 (10): 2513–22. https://doi.org/10.1016/j.asoc.2011.10.009.

The authors examine the performance of SVMs, a popular learning algorithm, in predicting the direction of the Nikkei 225 Index. Relative to forecasts obtained via linear discriminant analysis, quadratic discriminant analysis, and Elman backpropagation neural networks, forecasts reached via SVM are more accurate in predicting the direction of the stock index. The forecasting performance can be further improved by combining SVM with other classification techniques.

Huang, Zan, Hsinchun Chen, Chia-Jung Hsu, Wun-Hwa Chen, and Soushan Wu. 2004. "Credit Rating Analysis with Support Vector Machines and Neural Networks: A Market Comparative Study." *Decision Support Systems* 37 (4): 543–58. https://doi.org/10.1016/S0167-9236(03)00086-1.

The authors of this study apply SVMs to corporate credit rating analysis. Both the SVM and benchmark neural network techniques yield approximately 80% prediction accuracy for US and Taiwan market data. In addition, the authors implement input financial variable contribution analysis to help interpret the neural network results.

Hutchinson, James M., Andrew W. Lo, and Tomaso Poggio. 1994. "A Nonparametric Approach to Pricing and Hedging Derivative Securities via Learning Networks." *Journal of Finance* 49 (3): 851–89. https://doi.org/10.1111/j.1540-6261.1994.tb00081.x.

In this article, the authors present a nonparametric pricing approach for estimating pricing and hedging derivative securities. Unlike a parametric approach for estimating the arbitrage-based pricing formula, a nonparametric approach does not require that the dynamics of asset prices be known in advance. Using data on pricing and delta hedging of S&P 500 futures options, the authors find that in the majority of cases, a network-pricing formula outperforms the naive traditional Black–Scholes model. In addition, compared with other popular models—such as ordinary least squares, radial basis function networks, multilayer perceptron network, and projection pursuit—the neural network pricing formula is computationally more efficient and accurate when the price dynamics of the underlying asset are unknown.

James, Gareth, Daniela Witten, Trevor Hastie, and Robert Tibshirani. 2017. *An Introduction to Statistical Learning with Applications in R*. New York: Springer.

In this book, the authors provide a fundamental understanding of statistical learning, including LASSO, classification and regression trees, boosting, and SVMs. Unlike other textbooks in this new area, this one treats these topics in a less technical manner and focuses on their application using statistical software R.

Kaashoek, Johan F., and Herman K. van Dijk. 2002. "Neural Network Pruning Applied to Real Exchange Rate Analysis." *Journal of Forecasting* 21 (8): 559–77. https://doi.org/10.1002/for.835.

The authors apply neural network pruning to exchange rate forecasting. Because neural networks consist of many cells, the number of cells is pruned or reduced using basic descriptive procedures, such as multiple correlation coefficients, principal component analysis of residuals, and graphical analysis. Compared with standard autoregressive integrated moving average models, the proposed method performs better in terms of its predictive accuracy and its ability to capture the long-term dynamics of exchange rates.

Katona, Zsolt, Marcus Painter, Panos N. Patatoukas, and Jean Zeng. 2018. “On the Capital Market Consequences of Alternative Data: Evidence from Outer Space.” 9th Miami Behavioral Finance Conference 2018. https://ssrn.com/abstract=3222741.

The authors examine the use of satellite images of parking lot traffic to predict the earnings of major US retailers before public disclosure.

Ke, Zheng Tracy, Bryan T. Kelly, and Dacheng Xiu. 2019. “Predicting Returns with Text Data.” https://ssrn.com/abstract=3389884.

The authors propose a text mining methodology that extracts sentiment information from textual sources. This approach is simple, requires minimal computing power, and can be adapted to the dataset being used. A simple trading strategy that buys assets with positive recent news sentiment and sells assets with negative sentiment using this method generates higher out-of-sample abnormal returns than similar strategies based on sentiment scores from commercial vendors such as RavenPack.

Kearney, Colm, and Sha Liu. 2014. “Textual Sentiment in Finance: A Survey of Methods and Models.” *International Review of Financial Analysis* 33: 171–85. https://doi.org/10.1016/j.irfa.2014.02.006.

This article’s authors provide a comprehensive review of the text-based sentiment literature and qualitative information sources used in prior research, as well as the most frequently used textual data analysis methods and their empirical applications. Further, they identify possible opportunities and directions for future research using text-based qualitative data.

Kearns, Michael, and Yuriy Nevmyvaka. 2013. “Machine Learning for Market Microstructure and High Frequency Trading.” In *High Frequency Trading: New Realities for Traders, Markets, and Regulators*, edited by Maureen O’Hara, Marcos Lopez de Prado, and David Easley, 91–124. London: Risk Books.

The authors explore the application of ML approaches to high-frequency trading and microstructure data. They consider a few case studies used in solving different trading problems. Specifically, they review the application of ML methods in optimal trade execution problems and in predicting equity limit order book price movements.

Kercheval, Alec N., and Yuan Zhang. 2015. "Modelling High-Frequency Limit Order Book Dynamics with Support Vector Machines." *Quantitative Finance* 15 (8): 1315–29. https://doi.org/10.1080/14697688.2015.1032546.

The authors develop an SVM-based learning model to examine the dynamics of information contained in a limit order book. A limit order book records high-frequency trading activity grouped by asks and bids, including time and type of transaction, order price, and volume. The authors show the usefulness of features selected by the proposed method for forecasting short-term price dynamics.

Kim, Steven H., and Hyun Ju Noh. 1997. "Predictability of Interest Rates Using Data Mining Tools: A Comparative Analysis of Korea and the US." *Expert Systems with Applications* 13 (2): 85–95. https://doi.org/10.1016/S0957-4174(97)00010-9.

Forecasting techniques used in predicting interest rates have generally failed to improve over the simple random walk model. In this article, the authors consider neural networks, case-based reasoning, and the combination of the two to forecast interest rates in the United States and Korea. Case-based reasoning uses accumulated past experiences in making decisions. Interestingly, these techniques are superior to the random walk model for the US market but cannot outperform the random walk model for the Korean market.

Kirilenko, Andrei, Albert S. Kyle, Mehrdad Samadi, and Tugkan Tuzun. 2017. "The Flash Crash: High-Frequency Trading in an Electronic Market." *Journal of Finance* 72 (3): 967–98. https://doi.org/10.1111/jofi.12498.

The authors investigate intraday market intermediation in an electronic market around the time of large and temporary selling pressure that occurred on 6 May 2010. Known as the "flash crash," decline in prices and increase in trading volume was triggered by a trader who initiated a large sell program to sell E-mini S&P 500 stock index futures. This kind of large selling pressure may potentially lead to a market crash. Using empirical data from 6 May 2010 and the three days leading up to that date, the study finds evidence that most intraday intermediaries did not change their trading behavior despite large and temporary selling pressure.

Kirilenko, Andrei A., and Andrew W. Lo. 2013. "Moore's Law versus Murphy's Law: Algorithmic Trading and Its Discontents." *Journal of Economic Perspectives* 27 (2): 51–72. https://doi.org/10.1257/jep.27.2.51.

In this article, the authors survey algorithmic trading and its history, its major drivers, challenges, and the resulting unintended consequences for the financial system. They argue that although technological advances have reduced financial transaction costs drastically, current financial regulations need to be aligned with the requirements of the digital age.

Kofman, Paul, and Ian G. Sharpe. 2003. "Using Multiple Imputation in the Analysis of Incomplete Observations in Finance." *Journal of Financial Econometrics* 1 (2): 216–49. https://doi.org/10.1093/jjfinec/nbg013.

The authors examine the application of multiple imputation methods. When applied to two financial datasets involving severe data incompleteness, the imputation methods outperform the ad hoc approaches commonly used in the finance literature.

Kolm, Petter N., and Gordon Ritter. Forthcoming. "Modern Perspectives on Reinforcement Learning in Finance." *Journal of Machine Learning in Finance* 1 (1). https://ssrn.com/abstract=3449401.

The authors provide an overview of RL applications in finance. RL allows for solving dynamic optimization problems such as the pricing and hedging of contingent claims, investment and portfolio allocation, buying and selling a portfolio of securities subject to transaction costs, market making, asset–liability management, and optimization of tax consequences in a model-free way. The authors also highlight some of the challenges with using RL.

Kolm, Petter N., Reha Tütüncü, and Frank J. Fabozzi. 2014. "60 Years of Portfolio Optimization: Practical Challenges and Current Trends." *European Journal of Operational Research* 234 (2): 356–71. https://doi.org/10.1016/j.ejor.2013.10.060.

The authors review approaches that aim at addressing some of the practical challenges of portfolio optimization, including accounting for transaction costs, portfolio management constraints, and sensitivity to estimates of expected returns and covariances. They also illustrate several developments in portfolio optimization, including diversification methods, risk-parity portfolios, the mixing of different sources of alpha, and practical multi-period portfolio optimization.

Kumar, P. Ravi, and Vadlamani Ravi. 2007. "Bankruptcy Prediction in Banks and Firms via Statistical and Intelligent Techniques – A Review." *European Journal of Operational Research* 180 (1): 1–28. https://doi.org/10.1016/j.ejor.2006.08.043.

In this comprehensive review, the authors consider the application of statistical and intelligent techniques for bankruptcy prediction between 1985 and 2005. Historically, researchers have used many different techniques to forecast bank and firm bankruptcy, including traditional statistical methods, neural networks, case-based reasoning, decision trees, evolutionary approaches, rough set–based techniques, fuzzy logic, SVMs, and various hybrid models.

Lam, Monica. 2004. "Neural Network Techniques for Financial Performance Prediction: Integrating Fundamental and Technical Analysis." *Decision Support Systems* 37 (4): 567–81. https://doi.org/10.1016/S0167-9236(03)00088-5.

The author examines the effect of integrating technical and fundamental analysis to forecast the rate of return on common shareholders' equity. Empirical results show that a neural network incorporating financial statement and macroeconomic variables performs significantly better than the market return. It fails, however, to outperform the maximum benchmark—the average return of the top one-third of companies with the highest returns.

Leshik, Edward, and Jane Cralle. 2011. *An Introduction to Algorithmic Trading: Basic to Advanced Strategies*. Chichester, UK: John Wiley and Sons.

The authors of this book provide a background on algorithmic trading and describe current algorithmic trading strategies. The book contains two broadly defined parts. The first part is an introduction to trading algorithms, current popular algorithms, and how to use and optimize these trading algorithms. The second part provides readers with tools and examples to help them learn the trading strategies the authors have developed.

Leung, Henry, and Thai Ton. 2015. "The Impact of Internet Stock Message Boards on Cross-Sectional Returns of Small-Capitalization Stocks." *Journal of Banking & Finance* 55: 37–55. https://doi.org/10.1016/j.jbankfin.2015.01.009.

In this article, the authors study the stock return effects of stock messages posted on the Australian online stock message board HotCopper of the Australian Securities Exchange. The empirical evidence suggests that both the number of messages and their sentiment have a positive impact on the current return of underperforming small stocks and their trading volume. Large stocks, however, do not appear to be influenced by online message sentiment.

Li, Xiaodong, Xiaodi Huang, Xiaotie Deng, and Shanfeng Zhu. 2014. "Enhancing Quantitative Intra-Day Stock Return Prediction by Integrating

Both Market News and Stock Prices Information." *Neurocomputing* 142: 228–38. https://doi.org/10.1016/j.neucom.2014.04.043.

Previous studies on stock prices and market news consider either market news or past stock prices a predictor of future stock returns. In this article, the authors integrate these two sources of information using a kernel learning technique. The empirical evidence suggests that the proposed method outperforms three baseline models (market news, past stock prices, and both market news and past stock prices).

Liao, Shu-Hsien, and Shan-Yuan Chou. 2013. "Data Mining Investigation of Co-Movements on the Taiwan and China Stock Markets for Future Investment Portfolio." *Expert Systems with Applications* 40 (5): 1542–54. https://doi.org/10.1016/j.eswa.2012.08.075.

Taiwan and China signed an Economic Cooperation Framework Agreement in 2010. In this article, the authors investigate the co-movements in the two countries' stock markets after this agreement. To do so, they identify 30 categories of stock indices and analyze their behavior using patterns, rules, and cluster analysis. The empirical results show that for the Taiwan stock market, electronics, financial and insurance, and semiconductor stock indices strongly move together with the TAIEX Index. For the Hong Kong stock market, real estate, telecommunications, and financial services stock indices move with the HSI Index, and for the Shenzhen stock market, manufacturing, machinery, and electronics stock indices move with the SZSE Index. The authors also discuss the co-movement across these three stock markets.

Lin, Chin-Shien, Haider A. Khan, Ruei-Yuan Chang, and Ying-Chieh Wang. 2008. "A New Approach to Modeling Early Warning Systems for Currency Crises: Can a Machine-Learning Fuzzy Expert System Predict Currency Crises Effectively?" *Journal of International Money and Finance* 27 (7): 1098–121. https://doi.org/10.1016/j.jimonfin.2008.05.006.

In this study, the authors develop a hybrid causal model to predict currency crises. This hybrid model, constructed by integrating neural networks with a fuzzy logic model, can predict currency crises better than other popular methods, such as neural networks and logistic regression.

Lopez de Prado, Marcos. 2016. "Building Diversified Portfolios that Outperform Out of Sample." *Journal of Portfolio Management* 42 (4): 59–69. https://doi.org/10.3905/jpm.2016.42.4.059.

Markowitz's critical line algorithm (CLA) is based on quadratic optimization. The CLA procedure is unstable mainly because the algorithm requires the inversion of a covariance matrix. The authors introduce a hierarchical risk parity (HRP) method, an alternative algorithm that applies graph theory and ML, which uses the information in the covariance matrix without requiring a matrix inversion. By replacing the covariance matrix with a tree structure, the HRP method allows for solution of the portfolio optimization problem even when the covariance matrix is singular. Monte Carlo experiments show that HRP produces lower out-of-sample variance than does the CLA procedure, whereas CLA delivers minimum-variance portfolios only in sample.

Loterman, Gert, Iain Brown, David Martens, Christophe Mues, and Bart Baesens. 2012. "Benchmarking Regression Algorithms for Loss Given Default Modeling." *International Journal of Forecasting* 28 (1): 161–70. https://doi.org/10.1016/j.ijforecast.2011.01.006.

The existing literature on credit risk models focuses mainly on the probability of default, while loss given default (LGD) remains an inadequately studied area. The authors of this study consider numerous regression methods to model the LGD problem. Using data on losses from several major international banks, the considered models can explain 4% to 43% of the variation in LGD. Out of 24 models in the study, SVMs and neural networks perform significantly better than traditional statistical techniques.

Lowe, David. 1994. "Novel Exploitation of Neural Network Methods in Financial Markets." In *Proceedings of 1994 IEEE International Conference on Neural Networks*, vol. 6, 3623–28. Orlando, FL: IEEE.

The author introduces feedforward networks for portfolio management, demonstrating that neural network methods have the advantage of being able to approximate nonlinearities in the data and to optimize the portfolio under constraints.

Majhi, Ritanjali, Ganapati Panda, and Gadhadhar Sahoo. 2009. "Efficient Prediction of Exchange Rates with Low Complexity Artificial Neural Network Models." *Expert Systems with Applications* 36 (1): 181–89. https://doi.org/10.1016/j.eswa.2007.09.005.

In this article, the authors propose two ANN models—functional link ANN (FLANN) and cascaded functional link ANN (CFLANN)—to forecast currency exchange rates. They find that compared with Widrow's popular least-mean-square algorithm, both the CFLANN and FLANN models are superior in exchange rate forecasting, with the CFLANN model performing the best among the three models considered.

Manahov, Viktor, Robert Hudson, and Bartosz Gebka. 2014. "Does High Frequency Trading Affect Technical Analysis and Market Efficiency? And If So, How?" *Journal of International Financial Markets, Institutions and Money* 28: 131–57. https://doi.org/10.1016/j.intfin.2013.11.002.

Approximately 40% of foreign exchange traders use technical analysis for their trading rules, and others may implicitly rely on the efficient market hypothesis. In this article, the authors examine the relationship between technical analysis and high-frequency trading in foreign exchange markets. They develop a special adaptive form of strongly typed genetic programming to forecast most frequently traded currency pairs using high-frequency data. The results show that strongly typed genetic programming significantly outperforms traditional econometric forecasting models. Importantly, excess returns are found to be both statistically and economically significant, even when transaction costs are considered.

Manela, Asaf, and Alan Moreira. 2017. "News Implied Volatility and Disaster Concerns." *Journal of Financial Economics* 123 (1): 137–62. https://doi.org/10.1016/j.jfineco.2016.01.032.

In this article, the authors propose a text-based measure of uncertainty—a news implied volatility (NVIX) measure—to study the relationship between uncertainty and expected returns. Using front-page articles from the *Wall Street Journal* starting in 1890, the constructed NVIX measure captures the time variation in risk premia. Specifically, a high NVIX measure indicates high future returns in normal times and rises just before rare disaster events (e.g., wars, concerns about government policy, natural disasters).

Manning, Christopher D., and Hinrich Schütze. 1999. *Foundations of Statistical Natural Language Processing*. Cambridge, MA: MIT Press.

Statistical NLP applies probabilistic and information theory as well as linear algebra to characterize linguistic observations. This graduate-level textbook consists of four broad parts. Part 1 presents the essential mathematical and linguistic concepts. Part 2 focuses on word-based statistics and inference. Part 3 is devoted to studying grammar-based statistical techniques. Finally, Part 4 covers the applications of statistical techniques to NLP.

Markowitz, Harry. 1952. "Portfolio Selection." *Journal of Finance* 7 (1): 77–91.

In this seminal theory article, Markowitz describes the portfolio selection problem using expected returns and their variances. Also known as the mean–variance model, it chooses an efficient portfolio with the maximum expected return for a given level of risk.

McCarthy, John, Marvin L. Minsky, Nathaniel Rochester, and Claude E. Shannon. 2006. "A Proposal for the Dartmouth Summer Research Project on Artificial Intelligence, August 31, 1955." *AI Magazine* 27 (4): 12–14.

This article involves a republication of the seminal 1955 Dartmouth Summer Research Proposal on AI by four mathematicians. The authors of this research proposal are believed to have been the first to use the term "artificial intelligence." The authors suggested conducting a 10-man study on AI during the summer of 1956.

Michaud, Richard O., and Robert O. Michaud. 2008. *Efficient Asset Management: A Practical Guide to Stock Portfolio Optimization and Asset Allocation*, 2nd ed. Oxford, UK: Oxford University Press.

The authors discuss mean–variance portfolio optimization and its limitations, then review alternative portfolio management approaches from a statistical point of view. The topics covered include Markowitz efficiency, classic mean–variance optimization, traditional criticisms and alternatives, unbounded mean–variance portfolio efficiency, mean–variance efficiency with linear constraints, the resampled efficiency frontier and its properties, portfolio rebalancing and monitoring, input estimation, Bayes estimation and caveats, and avoiding optimization errors.

Mitkov, Ruslan, ed. 2014. *The Oxford Handbook of Computational Linguistics*, 2nd ed. New York: Oxford University Press. https://doi.org/10.1093/oxfordhb/9780199573691.001.0001.

This book is devoted to describing major concepts, methods, and applications in computational linguistics. It provides an overview of the field, describing a broad range of current techniques used in NLP and providing a comprehensive survey of current applications of NLP.

Molnar, Christoph. 2020. *Interpretable Machine Learning: A Guide for Making Black Box Models Explainable.* https://christophm.github.io/interpretable-ml-book/.

The author presents a free and comprehensive book on various ways of facilitating the interpretation and understanding of ML predictions.

Murphy, Kevin P. 2012. *Machine Learning: A Probabilistic Perspective.* Cambridge, MA: MIT Press.

The author of this advanced textbook on ML focuses on probability theory and distributions. The first part of the book is devoted to ML concepts and methods, probability theory and distributions, and Bayesian and frequentist statistics. The second part presents linear and logistic regression and generalized linear, mixture, and latent linear models. The third part discusses kernels, adaptive models (classification and regression trees, boosting, neural networks, ensemble learning), Markov and hidden Markov models, state space models, graphical models, variational inference, Monte Carlo inference, and DL.

Nevmyvaka, Yuriy, Yi Feng, and Michael Kearns. 2006. "Reinforcement Learning for Optimized Trade Execution." In *Proceedings of the 23rd International Conference on Machine Learning*, 673–80.

Optimized trade execution is an important problem in the field of finance. In this study, the authors apply RL to optimal trade execution using NASDAQ market data. When market state variables are chosen carefully, RL can improve trade optimization relative to other baseline execution strategies.

Nuij, Wijnand, Viorel Milea, Frederik Hogenboom, Flavius Frasincar, and Uzay Kaymak. 2014. "An Automated Framework for Incorporating News into Stock Trading Strategies." *IEEE Transactions on Knowledge and Data Engineering* 26 (4): 823–35. https://doi.org/10.1109/TKDE.2013.133.

The authors introduce a framework that automatically incorporates news into stock trading strategies. Using genetic programming to find optimal trading strategies, the authors achieve results that indicate that optimal trading strategies include technical trading rules and, in many cases, news variables as additional input.

Nuti, Giuseppe, Mahnoosh Mirghaemi, Philip Treleaven, and Chaiyakorn Yingsaeree. 2011. "Algorithmic Trading." *Computer* 44 (11): 61–69. https://doi.org/10.1109/MC.2011.31.

Trading in the financial sector uses automated systems that are fast and complex. In this article, the authors provide an overview of trading algorithms and how such systems work. In particular, the authors explain the trading objective, trading process, electronic trading execution, and trading analysis, and they provide some examples.

Oh, Kyong Jo, and Ingoo Han. 2000. "Using Change-Point Detection to Support Artificial Neural Networks for Interest Rates Forecasting." *Expert Systems with Applications* 19 (2): 105–15. https://doi.org/10.1016/S0957-4174(00)00025-7.

Interest rates change according to the monetary policy of governments, and the authors of this study propose to identify intervals between these change points and use this information in predicting interest rates. They use a backpropagation neural network (BPN) to detect the change-point groups of interest rates and apply the BPN technique again to interest rate forecasting. The proposed BPN technique with change-point detection outperforms the simple BPN technique at a statistically significant level.

Papaioannou, Georgios V., and Daniel Giamouridis. Forthcoming. *Enhancing Alpha Signals from Trade Ideas Data Using Supervised Learning, in Machine Learning and Asset Management.* Springer.

In this chapter, the researchers use trade investment ideas along with supervised ML. Trade ideas are market experts' recommendations that institutional investors often use. Investment trade ideas are classified into two classes (success or failure) using supervised ML methods, specifically random forests and gradient boosting trees. In addition to stock characteristics, the authors use characteristics of the contributor to the investment trade idea. The overall results demonstrate a performance improvement of more than 1% for long ideas and of more than 2% for short ideas.

Park, Saerom, Jaewook Lee, and Youngdoo Son. 2016. "Predicting Market Impact Costs Using Nonparametric Machine Learning Models." *PLoS One* 11 (2): 1–13. https://doi.org/10.1371/journal.pone.0150243.

Transaction costs affect the profits of investment strategies. The authors seek to more accurately predict market impact cost, which is the result of the difference between the initial stock price and the actual price after the transaction. Using data on the US stock market, the authors apply nonparametric ML techniques (neural networks, Bayesian neural network, Gaussian process, SVR) to predict market impact cost. The empirical results suggest that nonparametric ML models generally outperform their parametric counterparts.

Patel, Keyur, and Marshall Lincoln. 2019. *It's Not Magic: Weighing the Risks of AI in Financial Services.* London: Centre for the Study of Financial Innovation. http://www.csfi.org/s/Magic_10-19_v12_Proof.pdf.

The authors offer a detailed review of the potential benefits and risks of applying AI in the financial services industry. The report is divided into three sections. Section 1 introduces AI in the financial services industry. Section 2 discusses AI's potential benefits in financial services, such as improvements in security, compliance, and risk management. The report devotes much attention to Section 3, which presents the potential risks of applying AI and ML in financial services. It identifies 12 key risks, including those related to ethical challenges.

Peña, Tonatiuh, Serafin Martinez, and Bolanle Abudu. 2011. "Bankruptcy Prediction: A Comparison of Some Statistical and Machine Learning Techniques." In *Computational Methods in Economic Dynamics, Dynamic Modeling and Econometrics in Economics and Finance*, Vol. 13, edited by Herbert Dawid and Willi Semmler, 109–31. London: Springer. https://doi.org/10.1007/978-3-642-16943-4_6.

The authors examine the accuracy of statistical and ML methods in predicting bank failures. They introduce Gaussian processes for classification and evaluate the processes' performance relative to other statistical and ML techniques (logistic regression, discriminant analysis, least-squares SVMs). The study finds that forecasts generated from different instances of Gaussian process classifiers can compete with the results from popular techniques.

Rasekhschaffe, Keywan Christian, and Robert C. Jones. 2019. "Machine Learning for Stock Selection." *Financial Analysts Journal* 75 (3): 70–88. https://doi.org/10.1080/0015198X.2019.1596678.

ML methods are gaining in popularity among financial practitioners because they can better capture dynamic relationships between predictors and expected returns. Given the noisy historical financial data, however, the risk of overfitting poses a real challenge. The authors discuss two main ways of overcoming the overfitting problem when using ML for predicting the cross-section of stock returns. Combining different forecasts reduces noise. The authors recommend forecast combination along different dimensions, such as from different forecasting techniques, based on different training sets, and for different horizons. Similarly, feature engineering can help mitigate the overfitting problem by increasing the signal-to-noise ratio.

Rapach, David E., Jack K. Strauss, Jun Tu, and Guofu Zhou. 2019. "Industry Return Predictability: A Machine Learning Approach." *Journal of Financial Data Science* 1 (3): 9–28.

The authors apply ML to predict industry returns. Specifically, they use LASSO regression to fit sparse models that include lagged industry returns for 30 industries. The LASSO-selected variables are then estimated using an ordinary least-squares model to lessen the effect of downward bias in estimated coefficients from the LASSO model. In-sample and out-of-sample predictions of industry returns provide evidence for the relevance of information in lagged industry returns.

Rapach, David E., Jack K. Strauss, and Guofu Zhou. 2013. "International Stock Return Predictability: What Is the Role of the United States?" *Journal of Finance* 68 (4): 1633–62. https://doi.org/10.1111/jofi.12041.

Stock return predictability has received significant attention in the literature. In this study, the authors introduce a new powerful predictor of stock returns in industrialized countries. They find that lagged US market returns can dramatically improve stock return predictability in other industrialized countries, whereas lagged non-US returns are not good predictors of stock returns in the United States. The contribution of lagged US returns to stock return predictability in non-US industrialized countries is explained through a news-diffusion model, in which shocks to US stock returns are reflected in equity prices in other industrialized countries with a lag.

Renault, Thomas. 2017. "Intraday Online Investor Sentiment and Return Patterns in the U.S. Stock Market." *Journal of Banking & Finance* 84: 25–40. https://doi.org/10.1016/j.jbankfin.2017.07.002.

Using investor opinions and ideas about stock market returns posted on the *Stocktwits* blog, the authors construct investor sentiment data to study its relationship with US stock returns. They provide evidence that investor sentiment is an important variable for forecasting intraday stock index returns.

Ribeiro, Bernardete, Catarina Silva, Ning Chen, Armando Vieira, and João Carvalho das Neves. 2012. "Enhanced Default Risk Models with SVM+." *Expert Systems with Applications* 39 (11): 10140–52. https://doi.org/10.1016/j.eswa.2012.02.142.

Recent advances in bankruptcy prediction consider adding additional information, such as marketing reports, competitors landscape, economic environment, customers screening, and industry trends. This additional information can be incorporated into an SVM. Using data on French companies, the authors demonstrate that their adaptation produces a better bankruptcy prediction than does a baseline SVM.

Ristolainen, Kim. 2018. "Predicting Banking Crises with Artificial Neural Networks: The Role of Nonlinearity and Heterogeneity." *Scandinavian Journal of Economics* 120 (1): 31–62. https://doi.org/10.1111/sjoe.12216.

Early warning systems help predict coming banking crises. Rather than using traditional linear models, such as logistic regression, the author in this study builds early warning systems using an ANN model. For regional as well as international data, the proposed ANN model outperforms logistic regression in predicting all banking crises two years in advance, given the information about earlier crises.

Russell, Stuart, and Peter Norvig. 2010. *Artificial Intelligence: A Modern Approach*, 3rd ed. Upper Saddle River, NJ: Pearson.

The authors of this textbook provide an in-depth review of AI and cover introductory concepts as well as recent advances in the field. Topics include intelligent agents, problem-solving agents, search algorithms, logic agents, first-order logic and inference, planning, uncertainty in knowledge and reasoning, learning (e.g., learning from examples and learning probabilistic models), NLP and communication, and robotics.

Sabharwal, Chaman L. 2018. "The Rise of Machine Learning and Robo-Advisors in Banking." *Journal of Banking Technology* 2: 28–43. https://www.idrbt.ac.in/assets/publications/Journals/Volume_02/No_02/Chapter_02.pdf.

The author discusses the current use of ML and its future role in the financial sector. Robo-advisors used by the largest banks in the United States are examples that the financial sector has embraced ML for banking services. Still, ML has yet to achieve its biggest impact in the finance industry.

Schumaker, Robert P., and Hsinchun Chen. 2006. "Textual Analysis of Stock Market Prediction Using Financial News Articles." *AMCIS 2006 Proceedings*, 185: 1431–40. https://pdfs.semanticscholar.org/db74/80f28a68b95ed35701b84a282d6ebd8eb366.pdf.

The authors consider the impact of financial news on stock prices. Specifically, three textual document representations—bag of words, noun phrases, and named entities—obtained from news articles are considered. Using SVMs, the authors analyze the impact of news articles on stock prices 20 minutes after a news article is published. The study yields two interesting results. First, compared with linear models, the SVM finds that financial news has a statistically significant impact on stock prices. Second, various textual analysis approaches yield different stock return prediction performance. Compared with the popular bag of words, noun phrase textual representation results in better prediction performance.

Sevim, Cuneyt, Asil Oztekin, Ozkan Bali, Serkan Gumus, and Erkam Guresen. 2014. "Developing an Early Warning System to Predict Currency Crises." *European Journal of Operational Research* 237 (3): 1095–104. https://doi.org/10.1016/j.ejor.2014.02.047.

To predict currency crises in the Turkish economy, the authors use a financial pressure index—which measures drastic deviations in the exchange rate and drastic decreases in foreign exchange reserves—as the dependent variable and 32 macroeconomic variables as independent variables. The three models considered in this article—ANNs, logistic regression, and decision trees—are able to predict the 1994 and 2001 crises 12 months in advance and with 95% accuracy.

Simon, Dan. 2013. *Evolutionary Optimization Algorithms*. Hoboken, NJ: John Wiley & Sons, Inc.

This applied textbook, divided into five parts, is devoted to studying evolutionary algorithms for optimization. Part 1 discusses types of optimization problems and algorithms. Part 2 reviews natural genetics and their history and describes the use of artificial genetic algorithms for solving optimization problems. In Part 3, the discussion centers on related techniques, such as ant colony optimization, particle swarm optimization, and differential evolution. Part 4 is devoted to special types of optimization problems (discrete, constrained, and multi-objective optimization problems) and problems associated with reducing the computational costs of evolutionary algorithms. Finally, Part 5 provides a practical guide on how to address problems (checking for bugs and problems in the code and software) and how to measure the performance of an algorithm against standard benchmark optimization problems.

Skolpadungket, Prisadarng, Keshav Dahal, and Napat Harnpornchai. 2016. "Handling Model Risk in Portfolio Selection Using Multi-Objective Genetic Algorithm." In *Artificial Intelligence in Financial Markets: New Developments in Quantitative Trading and Investment*, edited by Christian Dunice, Peter Middleton, Andreas Karathanasopolous, and Konstantinos Theofilatos, 285–310. London: Palgrave Macmillan. https://doi.org/10.1057/978-1-137-48880-0_10.

The classical Markowitz (mean–variance) portfolio optimization model assumes that asset returns are normally distributed. In reality, means and volatilities of asset returns tend to vary, which requires forecasting these variables to construct an optimal portfolio. The authors present a solution to the portfolio optimization problem using a multi-objective genetic algorithm to account for the inaccuracy inherent in forecasting models. This model risk can be reduced when an approximation of the Sharpe ratio error of the portfolio of assets is added as an additional objective to the portfolio optimization task.

Sprenger, Timm O., Philipp G. Sandner, Andranik Tumasjan, and Isabell M. Welpe. 2014. "News or Noise? Using Twitter to Identify and Understand Company-Specific News Flow." *Journal of Business Finance & Accounting* 41 (7–8): 791–830. https://doi.org/10.1111/jbfa.12086.

Using 400,000 S&P 500 stock-related messages from Twitter, the authors compare company returns just before positive and negative news. Good news tends to have a larger information leakage and a greater impact on stock returns than bad news.

Tam, Kar Yan. 1991. "Neural Network Models and the Prediction of Bank Bankruptcy." *Omega* 19 (5): 429–45. https://doi.org/10.1016/0305-0483(91)90060-7.

Bank bankruptcy first increased significantly in the 1980s. The author uses a neural network technique to predict bank failure, showing that the proposed method performs better than traditional statistical methods in terms of robustness, forecast accuracy, adaptability, and explanatory capability.

Tan, Pang-Ning, Michael Steinbach, Anuj Karpatne, and Vipin Kumar. 2018. "Data Mining Cluster Analysis: Basic Concepts and Algorithms." In *Introduction to Data Mining*, 2nd ed., 525–603. New York: Pearson.

The authors provide an overview of cluster analysis and illustrate its application in different fields. In cluster analysis, data are partitioned into multiple groups or clusters that share some traits common within their group. The authors present different clustering techniques (e.g., K-means, hierarchical clustering) and discuss the strengths and weaknesses of various clustering methods.

Tan, Zhiyong, Chai Quek, and Philip Y.K. Cheng. 2011. "Stock Trading with Cycles: A Financial Application of ANFIS and Reinforcement Learning." *Expert Systems with Applications* 38 (5): 4741–55. https://doi.org/10.1016/j.eswa.2010.09.001.

The authors develop a new non-arbitrage algorithmic trading algorithm based on an adaptive network fuzzy inference system (ANFIS) and RL techniques. The proposed method predicts the changes in the long-term movement of prices and is able to outperform trading algorithms such as DENFIS and RSPOP. Experimental trading outcomes using five US stocks indicate that on average, total returns using the new framework are higher by approximately 50 percentage points.

Teräsvirta, Timo, Dick van Dijk, and Marcelo C. Medeiros. 2005. "Linear Models, Smooth Transition Autoregressions, and Neural Networks for Forecasting Macroeconomic Time Series: A Re-Examination." *International Journal of Forecasting* 21 (4): 755–74. https://doi.org/10.1016/j.ijforecast.2005.04.010.

The authors consider three techniques—linear autoregressive, smooth transition autoregressive (STAR), and neural network time-series models—to forecast macroeconomic variables. Using a dynamic model specification, the authors produce results indicating that the dynamic STAR model performs better than the linear autoregressive and several fixed STAR models in terms of forecast accuracy. Neural network models can produce more accurate forecasts when the forecast horizon is long and when the Bayesian regularization is applied to the model.

Tibshirani, Robert. 1996. "Regression Shrinkage and Selection via the Lasso." *Journal of the Royal Statistical Society. Series B. Methodological* 58 (1): 267–88. https://doi.org/10.1111/j.2517-6161.1996.tb02080.x.

The author introduces the LASSO method in linear regression models. By adding a penalty term to the mean squared error minimization problem, LASSO shrinks some coefficients to zero and produces models that are interpretable. Compared with other variable selection techniques, such as subset selection and ridge regression, LASSO is better suited for small- to moderate-sized numbers of moderate-sized effects.

Tsai, Chih-Fong, Yuah-Chiao Lin, David C. Yen, and Yan-Min Chen. 2011. "Predicting Stock Returns by Classifier Ensembles." *Applied Soft Computing* 11 (2): 2452–59. https://doi.org/10.1016/j.asoc.2010.10.001.

In this article, the authors compare the prediction performance of ensemble models of classification for stock returns. They find that relative to single classifiers, classifier ensembles perform well in terms of return on investment and prediction accuracy.

Tsai, Chih-Fong, and Jhen-Wei Wu. 2008. "Using Neural Network Ensembles for Bankruptcy Prediction and Credit Scoring." *Expert Systems with Applications* 34 (4): 2639–49. https://doi.org/10.1016/j.eswa.2007.05.019.

The authors compare the forecast accuracy of multiple neural network classifiers with that of a single best neural network classifier for bankruptcy prediction and credit scoring problems. The empirical results show that multiple classifiers tend to perform worse than a single best neural network classifier. If type I or type II errors are considered, however, neither method outperforms the other in terms of prediction accuracy.

Vapnik, Vladimir N. 2000. *The Nature of Statistical Learning Theory*, 2nd ed. New York: Springer. https://doi.org/10.1007/978-1-4757-3264-1.

The author reviews statistical learning for small data samples that do not rely on *a priori* information. The book, which is appropriate to be used as a graduate-level textbook on learning theory, is divided into three parts: the general theory of learning, support vector estimation, and statistical foundations of learning theory.

Varetto, Franco. 1998. "Genetic Algorithms Applications in the Analysis of Insolvency Risk." *Journal of Banking & Finance* 22 (10–11): 1421–39. https://doi.org/10.1016/S0378-4266(98)00059-4.

The author studies insolvency risk and compares results obtained from traditional linear discriminant analysis and genetic algorithms. Using data on Italian companies from 1982 to 1995, the author finds that linear discriminant analysis better predicts insolvency. The genetic algorithms produce results faster and with less contribution from the financial analyst, however, and can therefore serve as an effective tool in bankruptcy risk analysis.

Verikas, Antanas, Zivile Kalsyte, Marija Bacauskiene, and Adas Gelzinis. 2010. "Hybrid and Ensemble-Based Soft Computing Techniques in Bankruptcy Prediction: A Survey." *Soft Computing* 14: 995–1010. https://doi.org/10.1007/s00500-009-0490-5.

The authors review literature on hybrid and ensemble-based soft computing techniques used in bankruptcy prediction studies. Because the literature on bankruptcy prediction rarely reports confidence intervals of prediction results, and studies use vastly different data, comparisons of the obtained results are not feasible. Instead, the authors focus on specific techniques and their ensembles used in bankruptcy prediction.

Vui, Chang Sim, Gan Kim Soon, Chin Kim On, Rayner Alfred, and Patricia Anthony. 2013. "A Review of Stock Market Prediction with Artificial Neural Network." In *2013 IEEE International Conference on Control System, Computing and Engineering (ICCSCE)*, 477–82.

ANN can be a useful technique for stock market prediction, given the nonlinear and volatile nature of stock market dynamics. The authors provide a brief review of the literature on the application of various ANN approaches in predicting stock market returns.

Xing, Frank Z., Erik Cambria, and Roy E. Welsch. 2018. "Natural Language Based Financial Forecasting: A Survey." *Artificial Intelligence Review* 50: 49–73. https://doi.org/10.1007/s10462-017-9588-9.

In recent years, the number of papers using textual sentiment data for financial forecasting has been increasing. The authors review the natural language based financial forecasting literature, discussing the history of NLP techniques, current text processing techniques, and algorithms for predictive models.

Xue, Jingming, Qiang Liu, Miaomiao Li, Xinwang Liu, Yongkai Ye, Siqi Wang, and Jianping Yin. 2018. "Incremental Multiple Kernel Extreme Learning Machine and Its Application in Robo-Advisors." *Soft Computing* 22: 3507–17. https://doi.org/10.1007/s00500-018-3031-2.

Robo-advisors currently used in the finance industry provide investors with financial advice previously provided by finance sector employees. The authors suggest that the ML algorithm robo-advisors use may be less suitable when information is heterogeneous. They introduce an incremental multiple kernel extreme learning machine model, which can initialize and simultaneously update the training dataset and combine information from different data sources. The proposed method is able to efficiently solve classification problems and can thus be used as an algorithm for robo-advisors.

Yao, Jingtao, Yili Li, and Chew Lim Tan. 2000. "Option Price Forecasting Using Neural Networks." *Omega* 28 (4): 455–66. https://doi.org/10.1016/S0305-0483(99)00066-3.

The authors of this study use a neural network option pricing model and show that the proposed approach achieves different performance results depending on how data are partitioned into groups based on moneyness. Using Japanese Nikkei 225 Futures data, the authors find that a neural network pricing model outperforms the Black–Scholes model when markets are volatile, whereas the latter performs better when its theoretical assumption of constant volatility holds. The traditional Black–Scholes model performs better for at-the-money options. For in-the-money and out-of-the-money options, a neural network pricing model may be more appropriate when the preferred strategy is high risk and high return.

Yu, Lean, Shouyang Wang, and Kin Keung Lai. 2008. "Neural Network-Based Mean–Variance-Skewness Model for Portfolio Selection." *Computers & Operations Research* 35 (1): 34–46. https://doi.org/10.1016/j.cor.2006.02.012.

Researchers have been studying extensions of Markowitz's mean–variance model of portfolio optimization. Recent work in this area recommends incorporating higher-order moments, such as skewness, especially when asset returns are not normally distributed. The authors of this study present a neural network–based mean–variance-skewness model of portfolio optimization. They integrate this model with investors' risk preferences, different forecasts, and trading strategies and show that the proposed algorithm is computationally fast and efficient in solving the triple trade-offs in the mean–variance-skewness portfolio optimization problem.

Yu, Lean, Shouyang Wang, Kin Keung Lai, and Fenghua Wen. 2010. "A Multiscale Neural Network Learning Paradigm for Financial Crisis Forecasting." *Neurocomputing* 73 (4–6): 716–25. https://doi.org/10.1016/j.neucom.2008.11.035.

The authors propose a novel approach to predicting exchange rates. They develop a multiscale neural network learning algorithm for the exchange rates, which are decomposed into multiple independent intrinsic mode components using the Hilbert EMD (empirical mode decomposition) algorithm. The findings show that the new EMD-based multiscale neural network learning approach performs well in forecasting bank crises and is superior to other classification methods.

Zetzsche, Dirk A., Douglas W. Arner, Ross P. Buckley, and Brian W. Tang. 2020. "Artificial Intelligence in Finance: Putting the Human in the Loop." CFTE Academic Paper Series: Centre for Finance, Technology and Entrepreneurship, no. 1; University of Hong Kong Faculty of Law Research Paper No. 2020/006. https://ssrn.com/abstract=3531711.

The authors develop a regulatory roadmap for the use of AI in finance, focusing in particular on human responsibility and highlighting the necessity of human involvement. After describing various cases of AI's use in finance, the authors discuss a range of potential issues, then consider the regulatory challenges and tools available. The key issues identified are increased information asymmetries, data dependencies, and system interdependencies leading to unexpected consequences.

Zhang, Gioqinang, and Michael Y. Hu. 1998. "Neural Network Forecasting of the British Pound/US Dollar Exchange Rate." *Omega* 26 (4): 495–506. https://doi.org/10.1016/S0305-0483(98)00003-6.

Numerous studies successfully apply neural networks to exchange rate forecasting. In this study, the authors look at the impact of the number of parameters to be estimated on exchange rate forecasting because neural networks require the estimation of many parameters. Using the GBP/USD exchange rate forecasting problem as an empirical exercise, the authors find that the number of input nodes and hidden nodes affects the forecasting performance of neural networks.

Zhang, Guoqiang, Michael Y. Hu, B. Eddy Patuwo, and Daniel C. Indro. 1999. "Artificial Neural Networks in Bankruptcy Prediction: General Framework and Cross-Validation Analysis." *European Journal of Operational Research* 116 (1): 16–32. https://doi.org/10.1016/S0377-2217(98)00051-4.

The authors provide a comprehensive review of neural network methods used in bankruptcy prediction studies and find that these methods are superior to logistic regression models in bankruptcy forecasting and classification. The authors explain that the superior performance of neural networks results from their link to Bayesian posterior probabilities.

Zheng, Ban, Eric Moulines, and Frederic Abergel. 2013. "Price Jump Prediction in a Limit Order Book." *Journal of Mathematical Finance* 3 (2): 242–55. https://doi.org/10.4236/jmf.2013.32024.

The authors study the empirical relationship between bid–ask limit order liquidity balance and trade direction and the usefulness of information contained in limit order books. The results show that bid–ask liquidity balance helps to predict the direction of the next trade. Further, the authors examine the intertrade price jump using logistic regression, where the most informative features in limit order books are selected by the LASSO variable selection technique. Empirical results using data on French stocks show that trade sign, market order sign, and liquidity on the best bid–ask are all important factors for price jump prediction.

Zimmermann, Hans Georg, Ralph Neuneier, and Ralph Grothmann. 2002. "Active Portfolio-Management Based on Error Correction Neural Networks." In *Advances in Neural Information Processing Systems 14*, edited by Thomas G. Dietterich, Suzanna Becker, and Zoubin Ghahramani, 1465–72. Cambridge, MA: MIT Press.

In this study, the authors combine the Black–Litterman portfolio optimization model with neural networks to forecast excess returns. The forecasts of the expected return are based on error correction neural networks that use the previous model's error. Using data from 21 financial markets in G–7 countries, the proposed portfolio optimization model is shown to outperform a benchmark portfolio.

Named Endowments

The CFA Institute Research Foundation acknowledges with sincere gratitude the generous contributions of the Named Endowment participants listed below.

Gifts of at least US$100,000 qualify donors for membership in the Named Endowment category, which recognizes in perpetuity the commitment toward unbiased, practitioner-oriented, relevant research that these firms and individuals have expressed through their generous support of the CFA Institute Research Foundation.

Ameritech
Anonymous
Robert D. Arnott
Theodore R. Aronson, CFA
Asahi Mutual Life Insurance Company
Batterymarch Financial Management
Boston Company
Boston Partners Asset Management, L.P.
Gary P. Brinson, CFA
Brinson Partners, Inc.
Capital Group International, Inc.
Concord Capital Management
Dai-Ichi Life Insurance Company
Daiwa Securities
Mr. and Mrs. Jeffrey Diermeier
Gifford Fong Associates
Investment Counsel Association of America, Inc.
Jacobs Levy Equity Management
John A. Gunn, CFA
John B. Neff, CFA
Jon L. Hagler Foundation
Long-Term Credit Bank of Japan, Ltd.
Lynch, Jones & Ryan, LLC
Meiji Mutual Life Insurance Company
Miller Anderson & Sherrerd, LLP
Nikko Securities Co., Ltd.
Nippon Life Insurance Company of Japan
Nomura Securities Co., Ltd.
Payden & Rygel
Provident National Bank
Frank K. Reilly, CFA
Salomon Brothers
Sassoon Holdings Pte. Ltd.
Scudder Stevens & Clark
Security Analysts Association of Japan
Shaw Data Securities, Inc.
Sit Investment Associates, Inc.
Standish, Ayer & Wood, Inc.
State Farm Insurance Company
Sumitomo Life America, Inc.
T. Rowe Price Associates, Inc.
Templeton Investment Counsel Inc.
Frank Trainer, CFA
Travelers Insurance Co.
USF&G Companies
Yamaichi Securities Co., Ltd.

Senior Research Fellows

Financial Services Analyst Association

For more on upcoming Research Foundation publications and webcasts, please visit www.cfainstitute.org/en/research/foundation.

Made in the USA
Las Vegas, NV
08 November 2026

57691394R00059